How Do You Know When It's God?

Jeanice Sherai Durrah

JEANICE SHERAI DURRAH

Copyright © 2022 Jeanice Sherai Durrah

All rights reserved.

ISBN:
ISBN-13:

DEDICATION

This book is dedicated to every single woman who has felt God tugging on her to take a journey into something new. It is for every woman who has wondered along the way, "Is this God?" This book was written with you specifically in mind! May every question you have within be answered as you continue forward on your journey and may this book be utilized as a helpful tool on that journey.

JEANICE SHERAI DURRAH

ACKNOWLEDGMENTS

I would like to thank my husband, Victor Durrah, Jr. He is not only my partner in life, but also my partner in faith. Thank you for always encouraging me to believe in what God has placed within me. I would also like to give a special thank you to our daughter, Victory Durrah. In Victory's eleven months of life, she has taught me more about seeking God in prayer and leaning my ear to hear Him, than anything else has in my life. Many thanks to my parents, Mr. and Mrs. George & Patsy Casey, who raised and taught me to always allow my life to be set upon the foundation of Jesus Christ. Without their teaching and this foundation, I would be constantly lost with no clue as to who to turn to for direction. I am grateful for every single person who contributed to the success of this book. Your questions over the years have equipped me with the wisdom I needed in order to answer those questions for others who may be wondering the very same things. Last, but definitely not least, I would like to acknowledge my editor and sister, Denise Casey. Thank you for your continued commitment to my writings.

FOREWORD

If you have ever wondered whose voice, you are hearing or whose directions you are following. Sherai has hit the bulls' eye in this book, the target being what to expect and how to handle it. A careful reading of this book will weed out those voices of the evil one and those of your own. As Sherai illustrates, God's voice will align with His Word. There is no shortcut to following the mission He has for you. This book makes clear the voice and the stops to complete the mission. It also explains there is no hurry. Take your time because usually, when this is complete, we must do something else. Sherai is a chosen vessel to deliver God's message to His people, but she realizes she must stay close to God through prayer, worship, and meditation to keep her grounded. She uses her experiences with humanity and interactions with God to help us navigate our missions with our Creator. After reading this book, not only will we know that God is speaking, but we will also be able to understand His language and recognize His voice. A must-read for all of us who desire a right and obedient relationship with God.

Written by: George M. Casey, Jeanice Sherai's Father

Table of Contents

INTRODUCTION 9

1 THE ENEMY AND OUR GIFTS 20

2 GOD AND HIS GRACE 25

3 IN THE CLASSROOM WITH JESUS 34

4 PRAY 45

5 THE MODEL PRAYER 56

6 A WALK THAT IS GUIDED 65

7 WHEN JESUS INTERRUPTS YOUR DAY 78

8 I DON'T KNOW WHERE TO GO 89

9 MEDITATE ON GOD'S WORD DAY AND NIGHT 100

10 A COFFEE DATE WITH JESUS 114

11 A GOD WHO IS ALWAYS SPEAKING 123

FINAL WORDS 150

Praise for
How Do You Know When It's God

"How Do You Know When It's God" by Jeanice Sherai Durrah is a thorough and thought-provoking book. This book takes a God seeker on a journey to self-discovery, not only by providing helpful tools that encourage curiosity and introspection but also by taking the reader's hand and walking step-by-step through what God is saying. Durrah's willingness to be candid and vulnerable throughout allows for a beautifully relatable transformation through God. She shares knowledge, understanding, and experience in a masterful book that can enrich readers' walk with Christ greatly. Durrah provides her readers with journaling space for self-reflection, strategy, and evaluation throughout the book. Each chapter is like a walk on a journey to find out how to get closer and closer to God's plans for our lives. This book is very informative and applicable. God's Word backs Durrah's thought leadership, and as creative, as her writing might seem, Durrah has done a great job citing the Word of God throughout the book. Not only does Durrah give sound application, but she is very intentional about giving the reader real-life examples to which we all can relate, making this read more transformative and personable. If you are looking for an excellent guide, journal, and testimonial to help you better understand God's voice over your life, this is the book for you.

Written by: Victor Durrah, Jr., Jeanice Sherai's Husband

INTRODUCTION

But if you are led by the Spirit, you are not under the law.
Galatians 5:18 ESV

My Why
For the latter part of my years, there has often been this one question that I continuously get, "**How do you know when it's God?**"

I remember when I first began to get this question from those around me. My immediate response would be ***offense***. You see I was traveling on a journey that didn't make sense. I had stepped on to a path that was away from what I was currently doing, yet I knew *within* me that where I was going, God was **leading** me.

Even though it *appeared* in the "physical," that my decision to follow where I believed God was leading made no sense.

Long before my decision was made, I could feel God speaking to me about my current assignment. I could hear the winds of change all around me, but even then, I knew as God prepared me, it was not yet time.

When it was time, I **knew**. I knew with everything within

me that what **God** had called me to do in that season was completed and **now** it was time for me to pass the torch.

Yes, there was work to be done, but my part of the work was finished. We all tend to hang on to assignments in life for years when God has only called "some" of us to those assignments for a **season**.

So, when I *started* this journey, it *appeared* that I was <u>extremely</u> confident, but the reality is... I was shaking **tremendously** on the inside.

Fear had engulfed and overwhelmed me.

I was so afraid of stepping outside of God's will.
I was so afraid of getting it wrong.
I was so afraid of not doing what God was leading me to do.
I was so afraid of being disobedient.
I was *so* **afraid**.

Fear had consumed me and it began to take the lead in my life. I was now in the passenger seat of my journey, and somehow without me knowing it, fear had begun to drive.

The funny thing is... I don't think that those around me **truly** witnessed my fear when they looked at my journey. Even if they didn't *truly* understand what was going on, I think most **still** viewed my journey as one that was filled with both confidence and courage.

They didn't have a clue that *within* me, I was **constantly** questioning, *if* **this** *was truly* **God**.

"God are you sure? Is this truly You? Is this what YOU are calling ME to do?"

> **Question to Consider:**
>
> **Are you prepared to be vulnerable enough to take the risk of getting it wrong sometimes in life when determining when it's *truly* God?**

Following God is a faith walk and we won't ever know with **full** certainty if the path that we are on is *truly* God, but that one step in faith will **teach** us the ways that God leads in a way that standing still, **never** will.

On our personal life journeys of faith, we will have many spectators with many opinions. We have to understand that these spectators can only see the external actions that God is instructing us to take. They won't be able to visually see the internal battles we are fighting to stay focused and faithful on this journey. They will **only** be able to see the decision we made and the **impact** that decision will have on our life and sometimes the effect that it will even have on theirs.

They **will** ask questions, but their questions are not always out of just simply "being nosey" or to "ridicule" us. Those around us may **truly** be interested in how they too can walk out **their** own personal journey in life.

They are seeking us for answers because they've witnessed our steps and in the same way that they can't see our internal battles, we won't be able to see theirs.

Their questions are rooted in the need for **guidance**, for **help**, for **assurance**, and for **understanding.**

They desire to know what **we** went through so that they too can face the battles that they will face as they follow the path that God will call them to in their own life.

For me, when I stepped out to follow what I believe God had spoken, it became a *very* sensitive area for me. Here I was walking away from what was comfortable and normal to me into a calling on my life that I was not quite yet even aware of.

This is a faith walk, and when we walk by faith, we **very rarely will ever have sight** (2 Corinthians 5:7).

To be truthful, when I followed God, I *struggled* to believe that it *truly* <u>**was**</u> God, and although I was not verbally speaking that truth to others, my internal battles became **triggers** that were causing me to respond to everyone in a defensive manner.

> As they were questioning *me*, I was *literally* battling within those very **same** questions internally.

So, when people would ask me about my journey, I was triggered, and my mental battles would immediately begin.

I would wonder "Are they questioning **my** decisions? Are they trying to say that I don't *truly* **know** if it's God?" Instead of believing that the person asking these questions was truly asking to **receive** wisdom, the enemy would twist their questions in my mind and cause me to be defensive and divisive.

The enemy wanted me to believe that they were questioning *me* and what *I* had said and not *actually* seeking wisdom for ***their*** life and what God was speaking to **them** internally.

Sometimes I was right in the decisions I made that I thought were in complete alignment with God, but **a lot** of times I was **completely** wrong. So my pride, guilt, and shame were the ultimate **leader** of my thoughts and responses when they would turn to me for wisdom and advice.

Man!

I had **a lot** to learn and let me tell you, those lessons were

exhausting and **hard**!

That's why I'm writing this book, so that I may help others on their journey with God through the lessons that I've learned on my journey with Him.

I want to share the lessons I learned along the way, so that others can potentially <u>avoid</u> the same mistakes I made.

Yet... who are **we** fooling?

We are warned about most lessons we learn, but we as humans tend to learn the **most** through our very own personal failures.

> We must understand **more** than **anything** that our journey to **knowing when** it's God **will** be <u>tested</u>.

The journey you will take with me through this book will be one that is to teach you and prepare you, **but <u>never</u> to defeat you.**

Even when you get it wrong, you cannot stop! You must pick yourselves UP and keep going! Those wrongs are also a part of your journey!

How will this Book Help?

So how will this book help **you** with **knowing** when it's God?

In this book, you will learn through **my** personal journey and experiences:
- the ways God speaks,
- the ways He can and will confirm His voice,
- the importance of developing a personal relationship with God,
- and you will gain an understanding, knowledge, and awareness concerning His current communication and language with each of **you, specifically**.

How does God normally speak to us, individually?

> We have to know *how* God speaks to us **first** in order to know *when* it is actually God speaking.

Do you ever feel a nudge in your gut when you've run completely out in a conversation?

I have (too many times to mention).

Have you ever been going somewhere with friends, but suddenly felt like you should just stay home? What did you do? Did you understand why you had that feeling later?

Have you ever felt like you had the perfect job opportunity but something just did not seem right? How did you make the right decision?

We all, I am certain, have found ourselves wondering many times, "**How do I <u>know</u> when it's God?**" especially when facing tough or life changing decisions.

This book was written with the desire to not only answer that question, but also provide tools that will help each reader to develop their own personal relationship with God and provide the courage to believe when it is truly Him.

I pray that within the covers of this book, answers are found. I pray that once these answers are found, they are planted so deeply within each reader that by the time the last page is read, even if questions still linger concerning, "if it is God," that those questions will begin to be silenced and instead a TRUST is developed within, confirming, that you indeed *know* when it's God.

Following the Holy Spirit and receiving the guidance that has been prayed over, warred over, and prepared in **this** book on how do you <u>know</u> when it's God, will **require** faith to be exercised and the ability to "lean not on our own understanding (Proverbs 3: 5)."

It will require you to humble yourself and truly unlearn

what you've believed to be true in order to learn what God desires for you to know as the ultimate truth. It will require you to be open to **receive** something **new**.

It will require that your ears be prepared to **listen**, your heart be prepared to **receive**, and your hands be **ready** to do the work that will be required.

Are you ready? Do you believe that the Holy Spirit leads?

Then continue reading to learn, "**How Do You Know When It's God.**"

If you are reading this book and you're struggling to even understand who Jesus is, what is the Holy Spirit, and how does He even lead, I invite you to:

- Find your Bible, cell phone Bible app, or nearest computer and read the book of John in its entirety.
- Then, I ask that you pray (prayer is simply words we use to talk to God); ask God to lead a person to you that will help you to understand even more on this subject.
- If you do not know Christ as your Savior and you would like to develop a personal relationship with Him beginning today, simply repeat the prayer at the end of this chapter before you begin reading the remainder of this book.

God's Word promises that He will never leave us nor

forsake us (Deuteronomy 31:6).

He is a Good Shepherd.

I will not promise you that the path to Salvation and beyond is easy, but what I will promise you is that you will have a Savior who will indeed **keep** and **sustain** you no matter what you face in your life.

As I mentioned previously, God isn't looking for us to be perfect so don't even put that coat on, He knows how to do **His** work in those who are **willing** and He **desires** for all of us to live out our very **best** life.

The life He's always planned for us to live.

Format of this Book:

Each Chapter will have real life scenarios, biblical references, personal knowledge and wisdom on how the Spirit leads. You will have an exercise to complete, as well as a question to consider in each chapter. In some chapters, you will be invited to write a letter to yourself or someone else that is **led** by the Holy Spirit. Do not FEAR! God is with you and He **knows** why He led you to **this book.**

Salvation Prayer:
"Father, I come to you in the humblest manner asking for your love and forgiveness. I confess with my mouth that You are Lord and I believe in my heart that God raised You from the dead. Your word in Romans 10:9, tells me that if I do these things, then I am saved. Thank You God, for salvation and thank You for Your love. In Christ name, I pray, Amen.

1 THE ENEMY AND OUR GIFTS

"The easiest way to keep the enemy happy, is to never use our gifts."
~Jeanice Sherai

Did you know that the enemy wants to do **everything** possible to **keep** you from **using** your **gifts**?

Do you want to know **why**?

Because he knows that if he can convince you to not use your gifts, he can potentially stop **one** strategy or pathway that God intends to use to upbuild HIS Kingdom.

What do we know about the enemy? He is already **defeated**.
You cannot let his antics stop you.

WE KNOW HIS STORY!

> **The Enemy's Story (Ezekiel 28 & Isaiah 14)**
> Lucifer was a being created by God, that was known for leaving the creative hand of God in a perfect state. Yet, he became so engrossed with himself that he began to desire the honor and glory that belonged to God. Due to his prideful ways, he was tossed out of God's heavenly government, removed from his place of authority, and banned from living in Heaven. This punishment caused him to become corrupt. His name changed from Lucifer (*the morning star) to Satan (*adversary).

To accomplish this goal of limiting you in your gifts, the enemy will try every single tactic that he possibly can. If he cannot get you to doubt yourself, he will begin to use circumstances **and** *even* sometimes the people that you love, to make you doubt your value. Whatever he can do to make you feel ashamed, embarrassed, and guilty as you grow in your gifts, he will **try**.

While you are growing in your relationship with God, you will get things wrong... *a lot*.

I know, we are a prideful people that hate to get things wrong. We are a **self-righteous** people who would **rather** get everything **right**!

Yet, it is in *those* wrongs and those failures, that God has a way of teaching **us** what is **right**. No, we don't go out and **intentionally** plan to get things wrong. We are following the path that we **believe** is led by God with a faithful heart and blinded sight.

The enemy's goal is to persistently taunt you with what you have gotten wrong *before,* so that you never take a chance and never **move** from where you are currently in life.

He would rather attack you and ridicule you in a way that causes your self-esteem to fall so low that you decide to **never** follow or **trust** God again in your life. If you make that decision, the result is simple, you end up choosing to remain in the same place… **stagnant, afraid, and never moving.**

You will find yourself waiting stagnantly and passively in limbo, *hoping* that God will speak to you in *another* way.

Yet within, you *know* His instructions, you **recognize** what He said to do, but fear and pride causes you to believe that you **don't** know what He is instructing and that you don't know the way He is leading you to take.

> ### Take A Moment to Journal
>
> Write about a place currently in your life where you are stuck. How did this chapter on how the enemy does not want us to use our gifts help you to realize that it really *is* God, that's leading you?

_____

_____

_____

_____

_____

_____

2 GOD AND HIS GRACE

"The enemy may come to 'steal, kill, and destroy (John 10:10)' your life, but he can never beat out the faithfulness of God's Grace and His plan."
~Jeanice Sherai

You now know what the enemy is up to and the best way to defeat *any* enemy, is to understand their strategy.

So now that you **know**, you can move **forward**.

Before any of us were even thought of in this world, God **knew** who we were (Jeremiah 1:5). He knew the purpose we would be called to on Earth and He established victory for that plan before we even could foresee it.

God not only knew us, but He sent His Son to this world to save **each** of us (John 3:16). Jesus was sent to this earth for a **purpose** and when that purpose was fulfilled on the cross, He left us the best **gift** ever, and a Helper known as the **Holy Spirit.**

The **purpose** of the Holy Spirit is to **teach** us **ALL** things and **remind** us of the things that **Jesus** taught us as well (John 14:26).

When our minds are running rampant concerning our gifts and assignments, we have to stop and ask, "Who are we listening to?" Our fears, concerns and worries, *or* **our Helper**?

I can admit that my fears, concerns, and worries do tend to yell **extremely** loud, and that yelling can make it **extremely** hard to truly hear when my **Helper** is speaking, confirming, leading, and guiding me.

> **One of the key ways to determine "when it is God," is ensuring that when we approach Him, it is with a <u>pure heart</u>.**

It is *so* important that you recognize when your heart is dealing with turmoil. It is *so* important that you take the time to submit those thoughts, feelings, and emotions to God. It is *so* important that you listen to His wisdom in response to those things, so that you can be freed from **all** things that are not planted in you **by** Him.

Heart checks are necessary.

You must understand what is taking place within you because it is hard to truly know when it's God when our heart is filled with clutter, confusion, bitterness, and chaos.

There is no need for you to go to God:

- if you are not going to **trust** His response.
- if your mind is made up concerning what you will **<u>not</u> do**, *even* if He instructs it.
- if you have **malice** in your heart concerning a specific person.

If your heart is not pure, just wait!
You need to be able to hear <u>HIM</u>, <u>louder</u> than the things currently residing in your heart.

> The enemy knows how to speak to a heart that is filled with malice and "try" to **convince** you that what you heard **was** God.

If the voice you hear is:

- encouraging your anger,
- convincing you to believe that your actions were justified and right,
- producing fruit of selfishness and pride, and
- does not bear the fruit of the spirit (love, joy, peace, patience, kindness, goodness, and faithfulness).

That is not God.

We would *like* for God to be team **US** when we go to Him, but a lot of times, the very things frustrating us about others, situations, tests, or trials *is* God, Himself doing a needed work **within** us.

God tends to show us **ourselves,** before He will ever reveal the heart of others.

His Word in Matthew 7:3 (The Passion Translation) says, "Why would you focus on the flaw in someone else's life and yet fail to notice the glaring flaws of your own?"

God wants us to be more focused on the things separating us from Him (pride, anger, unforgiveness, addiction, selfishness, and more) than we are focused on pleading with or complaining to Him to "fix" that person that's frustrating or angering us.

The very things that He wants to work on within us internally are most times being mirrored externally right in front of us, and when that happens, we usually cannot stand it.

God challenges us to love when the world desires for us to hate. God challenges us to die to self, when circumstances are saying that we should pridefully deny people and honor ourselves.

God's ways are different from this world and what He requires of us is a true **stretch,** but the blessings of obedience will be more than we could ever think or imagine receiving in this life.

> **If you are experiencing emotions and want to know if they are truly of God, study the fruit of the Spirit.**

The fruit of the Spirit perfectly describes what God's voice should **immediately** produce in us: love, joy, peace, patience, kindness, goodness, faithfulness, gentleness, and self-control (Galatians 5:22-23).

What is that voice producing within you?

> Recognizing the **fruit** being produced **in** us as a result of the **voice** that we are hearing is one of the <u>**key ways**</u> to knowing *when* it's God.

Prior to approaching God for wisdom and direction it is important that you take time to worship, pray, and meditate on His Word so that when you **seek** Him, it is **HIM** on your mind and not the things plaguing you.

To understand God's voice, you must know His character, to know His character you must be knowledgeable of His Word. There are no shortcuts to knowing and understanding when it's God.

For many years I've spent every single one of my mornings, sometimes for hours at a time, in God's Word. Pouring over it, understanding His character, and wanting to learn more and more about how He speaks.

Knowing God's voice is not related to perfection. It's connected to the personal relationship that we each have with Him. God **does** speak <u>and</u> lead **imperfect** people. No matter how much others would like for us to feel condemned, the word imperfect describes **every single one of us that are living in this world**.

That is why God sent His Son. That's the grace we have inherited today by believing in Him.

So, at this point, if the thought that "God would **never** speak to me," is present, know that it is a lie originating from the enemy.

Chile! If you only knew the struggles I face currently! I too battle with unworthiness, but we serve a God who calls us worthy despite how this world would describe us and despite how we feel.

You must take off that cloak of perfection because you won't need it on this journey. Instead, you must put on the gift of God's grace and make sure that you put on your gloves of mercy because you will need it for others who are imperfectly walking out their journey as well.

I've spent a lot of time embarrassingly getting it wrong in order to truly understand and grow in my wisdom concerning what is and what is **not** God. The truth is, those lessons of getting it wrong will continue...even for me. We all are on a constant journey with God, and the journey will not be complete until we reach our final destination, which is **Eternity**.

Take A Moment to Journal

Write a Letter to yourself as if it came from a friend. Write about the places you feel guilty and the things you have not forgiven yourself for, but in this letter, extend yourself grace. Write it all down and at the bottom of your letter, write FORGIVEN. God has moved on from that part of your life, He is ready to do a brand-new thing (Isaiah 43:19). He is just waiting on you!

_____

_____

_____

_____

_____

_____

_____

_____

_____

_____

HOW DO YOU KNOW WHEN IT'S GOD?

3 IN THE CLASSROOM WITH JESUS

"I've learned that the life we live is one big classroom and it's up to each individual to truly apply the lessons."
~Jeanice Sherai

Imagine you are in a classroom with Jesus.

Jesus has just emerged onto the scene. He is the **hottest** preacher out on social media. I mean *everyone* has heard his story. They are amazed by His strength and how He consecrated Himself before God completely defeating the enemy.

You too are amazed by the stories you've heard. You've heard about the miraculous power that He has in His healing ministry, the authority and power that He speaks with on His ***many*** different platforms, and you are so **excited** to *finally* be able to attend His class**.**

I mean who *wouldn't* be?

This is an in-person sermon preached by Jesus, **Himself**.

The classroom is loud and buzzing with excitement as everyone waits in expectation to hear what He preaches on today.

A man in the classroom wants a miracle healing. He came with an addiction, and desires for God to take it away immediately. He has heard of Jesus delivering the people He has encountered with just one touch, and he is hoping this too will be his story upon leaving class today.

A woman wants Him to restore her marriage. She knows Jesus has the power to change and soften hearts, and she wants Him to speak a Word that restores her marriage immediately.

Someone else shows up desperately needing a breakthrough in their finances. They are tired of struggling and they recently heard the story of how Jesus blessed Peter in His business. They are hoping He can do the same for them in their life.

Why are **you** in this classroom?

Why did you show up to hear this sermon preached by Jesus today?

Really take time and **imagine** this classroom, the **anticipation**, the noise of people chattering excitedly.

Then imagine what would be <u>**your**</u> reason for showing up to hear Jesus on this day.

Take time to imagine the shift in the room when Jesus walks in, the immediate impact of His presence. Imagine a room going from loud chatter to utter and complete silence. What does His presence feel like to you in this classroom as He begins His sermon?

This classroom was **specifically** reserved for **you** and **every other person** that fills a seat in this room. He **knew** you would be here.

He also **knows** the power of prayer and He has been praying for you since God revealed that He would see you today.

He has been going over each of your prayers, reviewing them with God and now He is ready to **teach**.

He begins to preach to each of you that showed up with a **desperate** need, and what is His first lesson?

Jesus begins to teach on the **blessing** of dealing with hard things in life.

Here you sit in this classroom filled with anticipation, **thirsty** for a word that **delivers** you, and Jesus begins to preach on the blessing of being in a vulnerable/hard place at this particular time in your life.

You think to yourself, *"Did Jesus even **read** my prayer? I actually **need** Him in this moment! Why is He beating around the bush instead of just giving me what I **believe** I need as the answer to my current situation?"*

Take a moment to breathe, then ask yourself if you are sure that the answer you desire is **actually** the answer that you **need**?

Are you sure in this moment, that what your flesh is currently convincing you *is* the answer you're waiting on from God, *is* the **true** answer you need?

How much are you willing to submit to the God who knows **ALL** when it comes to Him answering your prayers?

There have been times I've gone to God about a co-worker, an associate, or literally anyone getting on my nerves and told Him that I'm ready to no longer deal with that person in my life and explained to Him that it was because they've truly gotten on my **last** nerve and He has, in response, led me to a scripture on **patience** (*rolls eyes).

I can honestly tell that you on those days, I would sometimes frustratingly close the Bible.

I didn't want patience, I wanted deliverance **out** of this mess, completely.

Yet, was deliverance from that place of development in my life what I *truly* needed?

> **In prayer, the Holy Spirit <u>always</u> leads. The question is, will your heart be positioned in a place where you are willing to follow.**

I'm sure at this point of the sermon, the man with the addiction is ready to get up and leave. He has prayed to Jesus fervently, begging God to deliver Him from this situation. He finally was able to obtain a seat in His nationally known seminar and Jesus is talking about the blessings in suffering and persecution.

This man wanted to be free from a thing that has cost him his life, his family, and almost everything except Jesus, and Jesus tells Him that this place is the **perfect** place to **be**?

Jesus is telling him that **this** place is where He should look to God with gratitude for His life instead of the disgust that he currently is feeling (**deep sigh*).

I can hear the thoughts of this man battling addiction, *"Maybe Jesus chose the wrong person to fill this seat for this particular seminar. Nothing about this place feels blessed, I need healing and deliverance!"*

Can you imagine the woman who showed up for a prophecy concerning her marriage? She has prayed fervently. Her name was **finally** chosen for the class.

Here she is in **this** classroom that **many** around the world desired to be in and Jesus shows up teaching on the blessing of being in mourning because it is in that place that Jesus will comfort you.

Is God serious? This woman came for a positive Word over her life, **not** a Word concerning the blessing of her tears and grief in this **very** hard place.

How would you feel?

What would be your reaction to Jesus?
Would you be angry?
Would you reject this teaching from God?
Have you been in a similar seat in the very same classroom being taught by Jesus?

You sit down to pray and tell Him about your problems and He in response reminds you that He has **always** told you that in this world there would be trouble (John 16:33).

Would you reject His teaching because it's not the teaching your flesh desires?

> **In prayer, the Holy Spirit <u>always</u> <u>leads</u> you through a process that will teach you as He heals you. You're showing up for a quick fix, but His response will always be related to what's needed for you in Eternity. There is <u>no</u> quick fix to your situation. He knows what's truly needed for you in THIS place.**

God wants to teach you strategy, endurance, and patience.

God wants to teach you lessons that will sustain you in the battles that you are facing. His word tells us in Romans 5:4 to be joyful when in times of trouble because those times produce patient endurance, and patient endurance refines our character, and a proven character leads us right back to **hope**.

> **Question to Consider:**
>
> If God chose to respond to your prayer by guiding you to instead see the blessings in your current situation, shouldn't we all realize and understand that our healing and deliverance is right there waiting for us in His message and that there is a shift in perspective that God wants in our life?

We desire healing that will immediately soothe our flesh, but Jesus is able to see **far** more than we can. He's not in it for a surface fix, He desires to do a **deep** cleaning of our souls.

If God does not **pluck up** at the **ROOT** what has been causing our current situation and problems, He knows that although the issues will be uprooted for a while, eventually those problems will begin to grow **again**.

He knows that unless it's a **root** work, your current situation would just be a constant cycle of failure, hardship, and heartache. You would be back at His feet again in the **very** same place.

Wouldn't you rather **learn** how to handle those hard circumstances versus asking God to give you temporary relief?

What about the next storm, which **will** come harder and much stronger, how will you handle that one if you don't grab the lessons that God is trying to teach you in this current place?

> "Trust God's process after YOUR prayer."
> **~Jeanice Sherai**

Jesus prepares your **heart** first.

He teaches you about your attitude of gratitude **even** in the storms. He prepares you for **any** storm you could face, not just your current one.

Then, guess what He does **next?** Instead of addressing your problem directly, He moves on to the next point of His sermon and begins to teach you about the blessing of fasting and giving.

By this time, you've had **enough**.

This was **not** why you showed up today!
Why is He skipping all over your prayer?
Is He even going to address our prayers individually?

Your thoughts are running rapidly and here is what you should **know**, as you sit in this classroom, Jesus *knows* what you are thinking.

He can hear the hardness of your heart as He continues to teach us vital lessons that we refuse to open our hearts to **receive**. The reason our hearts become so hardened is because when we go to God, we already have in our heart the answers we think that we **need**.

We tend to pray not to hear from God, but to get Him in agreement with what **we** believe is **best**.

> Recognizing the **fruit** being produced **in** us as a result of the **voice** that we are hearing is one of the <u>**key ways**</u> to knowing *when* it's God.

Your heart position is SO important in prayer.

Why do you think in this classroom, Jesus is first addressing the heart before he ever touches the prayer?

Why is he teaching you about your heart posture in tough times, during fasting, and during giving? Why is He driving the **long** way when a quicker way was way back there?

Jesus understands that in order to truly experience the magnificence of prayer, your heart **must** be set in the right position.

If you are going to God with your plans, when life has **repeatedly** shown you that this is **not** the way He planned for you to take. You will end up frustrated each time with

His response because while you are hoping God will change His mind, He is waiting for you to get in alignment with what He desires to truly do in your life in this season. God knows that no matter how much you pray to Him, if your heart is set in a different place, where you've already made up your mind on the answer you desire to receive you will be closed off to hearing what He is saying to you concerning your current situation.

> God will patiently wait until you trust His way enough to truly listen to His plan.
> ~Jeanice Sherai

It's funny because when we finally do things God's way and **see** the goodness and fullness of His plan, we wonder what in the world took us so long to be obedient.

The truth is most times we think we know more than **God** does about our life. God knows us better than our parents do and better than we know ourselves. His Word tells us, "Before you were in your mother's womb, I knew you (Jeremiah 1:5)."

How powerful is that? God knew us before we ever even came to earth. When we stepped on earth our story was **written**.

So why in the world do we argue with Him about what's best for our life?

4 PRAY

"Prayer is not just reserved for difficult moments; prayer is reserved for EVERY moment."
~Jeanice Sherai

There have been times in my life when words would not even surface in order for me to pray to God. Those were **deep** and **painful** moments.

There have been other times when I truthfully didn't even *want* the answer to the questions that were plaguing my heart. Those were moments where I had **high** hopes that **His** Will would **align** with **my** present desires (*deep sigh).

I'm not proud to admit that I have had moments in my life where I've desired **my** will more than **His**. I'm even less proud to admit that I can *still* have moments of avoidance concerning God's direction and **will** for my life.

Yet, who am I fooling?

If I am even *acting* in **avoidance**, I already *know* God's answer, **and** I am **perfectly** aware of **His** will.

Have you ever been there?
Do you still visit that place sometimes?
Have you ever parked there and just stayed?

How many of you know that obedience is **always** better than sacrifice (1 Samuel 15:22)?

God's way is *so* much better.
It just sometimes takes our human minds a little longer to **believe** Him concerning *that* way, and that is **okay.**

God knows **how** to get our attention.
That's why I truly believe that developing a habit of going to God in **prayer** for strategy, answers, clarity, and confirmation is **key**.

He **knows** the way that we should take and He's waiting for us to ask **Him** instead of continuing to try things our own way. God has gone **before** us, so He knows what's ahead **for** us.

Now, that doesn't mean that we will always receive the answers we need immediately. God operates on His time, not our time, unfortunately.

There have been times when I sought God **constantly** in prayer on a particular situation and in return **all** I would hear was silence. I mean day after day, *seeking* God, *crying* out to Him and in return...**Nothing**.

I **remember** when I first decided to follow God on my journey of healing and purpose. I believed that God had been speaking to me concerning His plan for over a year. I recognized that it was indeed Him leading me to my final decision through various things, including people speaking over me, and gifts that I received from the women of the church at the last women's conference that I hosted.

Yet, after conversations with the women of my church, my first lady, and my Pastor, it seemed that immediately, God became **extremely** silent. I would pray, God are you sure that this is where you're calling me? See in actuality, I had stepped out of a place of fruit and abundance into a season where I would begin wandering in the **wilderness.**

My manna and my water would not come from the places I would be accustomed to any longer (Exodus 16).

God began to pour those things into me from Heaven and quench my thirst with His Living water just like He provided the Israelites water from a rock.

I was in a different place in life and it was no longer about comfort, I was in a place that required me to have full and complete trust and **obedience**.

I remember seeking others for wisdom, but not really and truly getting the answers that I needed. The truth was that no one had the answers that I needed, **except** God. And my Father in Heaven...oh, He was **silent.**

Those were some of the **most** *frustrating* moments.

It's nothing like **needing** an answer from God and hearing absolutely **nothing**. What God used to fill me and answer me in that time would be enough to fill me for that day, but I wanted to be filled with enough that would carry me through my entire journey.

I would always hear older saints (and some younger ones too) asking, what **sin** is standing in your way? (*rolls eyes, begins to intensely search my heart and simultaneously takes a deep breath).

That question **always** got me because I honestly felt like, *"What sin are you specifically referring to because I thought we **all** sinned?"*

Have you ever been there? Trying to search your heart for sin and understand how **this** sin would stand in the way of your prayer?

> "I do believe that sin *can* in the spiritual realm keep us from hearing God, but sin *does not* keep God from hearing you."
> **~Jeanice Sherai**

So, while sin could be the very reason that I was not hearing my Father, it was not ever keeping Him from hearing the cries of His daughter. I realized that sin causes guilt and guilt can cause us to believe that we are not worthy to hear God, which in turn keeps us from truly being **open** to hearing Him.

I also realized on this journey that the presence of **fear** will a lot of times be a **barrier** that is set before us to **keep** us from hearing the truth of what God is speaking to us in our situation.

Fear works to keep us from hearing God, but, God did

not give us a spirit of fear (2 Timothy 1:7) and so if HE didn't give us that spirit, who did?

Learn to recognize the fruit within you and know when that fruit was not birthed from God. Then pray that thing out of you before you even go to God and approach Him for what you need.

Sometimes we are simply not open to hearing God's answer because of stubbornness, fear, pride, and many other things.

When I couldn't hear God, it was because I was going to Him in a place of fear. I was afraid of getting it wrong. I was afraid of stepping off His course. I was afraid of missing the promises that He had for me and I approached Him with that fear instead of faith and in return God was silent.

In NeNe Leake's voice, "**He said what He said**."

It was then up to **me**, to be **obedient**.

Other times in my life, God was silent without me truly understanding why. He's sovereign and we won't always be able to understand the ways of God with 100% fullness until He opens our eyes completely in Heaven.

Sometimes God just wants us to trust Him even in His silence. Sometimes He's asking us to be still in silence and

still isn't always physical. Sometimes He's saying, "Rest your anxiety and worries, I am here, keep going."
Other times He wants you to physically rest and wait for His directions in His silence. Trust your Helper, the Holy Spirit, to **guide** you in those times.

Not every prayer I've prayed resulted in my answer being delayed. There have been times when I've prayed, looked up, and literally the answer was right there.

I call those moments "God-Moments" rare enough to blow your mind, but just often enough to allow your faith to grow.

Prayer has always been a constant in my life.

It has been the one topic that has continuously interested me. It's the one thing that I absolutely love doing for others, but that wasn't always my story.

It wasn't until I realized the **power** of prayer and the **way** God would speak to me **during** prayer that I realized that prayer wasn't an option, it is a **requirement** in my life, and I **must** invite others to come along with me on this prayer journey.

My faith and commitment to prayer is deeply rooted in being born into a Christian family. A family threaded with ancestors who, at times, their **only** option was to pray. Ancestors who lived and fought so that I could live and

continue the fight. Those ancestors began a legacy of faith and prayer that has been deeply woven through out my family. They raised a lineage of powerful men and women who **knew** that the **key** to life was **indeed** prayer.

I was covered in prayer by my dad, mom, grandmothers, grandfathers, aunts, uncles, and so many more people in my life, and as the famous quote goes, "their prayers are *still* covering me."

> Prayer is key and it always will be the key that unlocks the secrets of the kingdom of God in my life.
> **~Jeanice Sherai**

I hope as you read this chapter, you held on to the keys.

We should ALWAYS have an open line of communication with our Savior.

If you are unsure of:
- your path,
- the next step to take,
- what decision to make, or
- if that person is *actually* good for your life,

You will have to talk to God, and you will have to learn to **listen to God**.

> "Prayer is going to be the key that opens the door to God's truth concerning those current situations in your life."
> **~Jeanice Sherai**

You will have to hear **Him** above your current feelings and in situations where your feelings are running rampant and uncontrollable. Know that hearing God in those situations can be **very** hard.

> **Silence the Chaos and Listen**
>
> Find A Quiet Place
>
> Breathe (Inhale & Exhale)
>
> Pick one Word to keep you Present
>
> Pray: Ask God to use that Word to Speak to you
>
> Listen.
>
> **Note**: Ignore fear, worry, doubt, and anything else that does not feel like **Peace**.

Did you know that there is an order to prayer?

One of the very first lessons I learned on my journey after stepping out and following God away from my Women's Ministry is that **order** is important. I attended a church with a very prominent woman who was a preacher. I loved the church, and more than that, I loved her sermons.

She was raising up a kingdom of women to step onto platforms that she had conquered. I believe she was raising them up to go even higher than she had. I noticed how these women adhered to her order of things. How they followed her teachings and served her in the capacity needed as she delivered the word of God.

I thought in my very early and very prideful days, "that could *never* be me." I struggled with **order**. I remember once approaching her and asking how could I serve in her church because I was a girl who was raised to not sit still in the church, **you served.** I remember her answer vividly and it turned me away because it was coupled with religious rules.

When I look back, I knew that the very first lesson God taught me, was about His divine order and how order is important in all that we do.

What a tough lesson to endure!

Have you ever paid attention to the way prayer is done in the Bible? There are one sentence prayers in the Bible, there are long prayers in the Bible, we are even taught to moan when we have no words to pray.

There is so much instruction for us on how to pray, yet I believe that the **order** in which Jesus taught His disciples to pray was purposed and VERY strategic.

I mean what else would we expect from Jesus *except* a detailed, successful strategy on how to pray?

5 THE MODEL PRAYER

"Prayer is the communication language that we use to speak with Jesus."
~**Jeanice Sherai**

Prayer is the communication pathway that we use to speak directly to our Father. There are many examples of prayer in the Bible to guide us. Prayer can be one word or many words. It is honestly based on your relationship with Jesus and what you are feeling in that day.

I want to teach you the order that Jesus taught His disciples concerning going to God in prayer.

Jesus teaches His disciples this order in Matthew 6, but **only** after He teaches them the correct way that their hearts should be **positioned**.

A Prayer to God
Modeled after Matthew 6:9-13 CSB

1. **Reverence God.**
    "Our Father in Heaven, Your name be honored as Holy."

My Example:
Dear God! You are Above all and You Created All! How Holy is Thy Name above all the Earth!

Your Turn:

_____
_____
_____
_____

2. **Pray for His Will and Purpose.**
   "Your Kingdom come. Your will be done on earth as it is in Heaven."

My Example:
Father, I only want your will and purpose for my life. Allow your will to be done and your Kingdom to come on earth as it is in Heaven.

Your Turn:

_____

_____

_____

_____

3. **Pray for Wisdom, Supplement, and the Things you need.**
   "Give us today our daily bread."

My Example:
Today I am asking for a Word from you on this situation and a confirmation that you know I will recognize and receive. Lead me Father in the way you would have me to go. Please supply my every need in this day. Open doors that I never imagined.

Your Turn:

_____

_____

4. **Ask for Forgiveness.**
   "And forgive us our debts, as we also have forgiven our debtors."

My Example:
Father please do not allow any sin to separate me from you in this prayer. Forgive me of my sins Father and show me any unforgiveness that is currently on my heart so that I may also forgive others.

Your Turn:

5. **Pray for Protection.**
   "And do not bring us into temptation, but deliver us from the evil one."

My Example:
Father, please keep me from temptation, do not let the enemy lead me astray. Keep me protected as I enter this day and protect my family. Guard us throughout this day.

Your Turn:

_____
_____
_____
_____

6. Conclusion.
"For Thine is the Kingdom, the Power, and the Glory. Amen"

My Example:
For God you are Mighty and Your promises are true. I lift my eyes to You in expectation. In Jesus' Name I pray, Amen.

Your Turn:

_____
_____
_____
_____

> When we go to God in prayer, we should **already know** that He has the answers. This isn't a fearful prayer. This is a **bold** prayer to an **All**-Powerful God. We must **know** that He **can** do it. The question is, is it in His perfect **WILL** to do it and that's what we are seeking...**HIS WILL.**
> ~Jeanice Sherai

Challenge: Pray for someone else today using the example above that you used to pray for yourself.

The Prayer for The Person You Chose:

_____
_____
_____
_____
_____
_____
_____
_____
_____
_____
_____
_____
_____
_____

A̲LLOWING THE H̲OLY S̲PIRIT TO L̲EAD YOU IN PRAYER

1) **Do your Research!**
   a) Learn the many ways that the Holy Spirit leads in prayer.
   b) Learn the many ways to pray.
   c) Study the examples of Prayer that you see in the Bible.
   d) Pay attention to the prayers of your Pastors and wise counsels around you.
   e) Ask questions about prayer as you continue to go deeper.
   f) Ask God to continuously reveal more to you on how He leads through prayer.

2) **If your heart is not in the right place, address your heart issues FIRST** (i.e., if you are praying for a friend, but you're at odds with him or her, clear that up **first**.

That way your answer will be based on God and not on what's currently going on in your heart). We are human, so things happen, but God can heal that place so that you can be free from that burden and be able to **hear** Him clearly.

3) **Once your heart is in the right place, PRAY!**

> **In prayer, the Holy Spirit <u>always</u> leads a heart that is willing, ready, and <u>set</u> in a position to trust, receive, and be obedient to His Will.**

<u>H</u><u>OW TO ENSURE YOUR HEART IS IN THE RIGHT PLACE</u>

1. **Fast:** The Bible shows us so many examples of individuals who gathered in groups to fast or who simply fasted individually in order to **truly** hear from God concerning a situation. Fasting is when we make physical sacrifices to spiritually grow closer with God. Fasting removes distractions so that you can truly develop a more intimate relationship with God and recognize who He is in your life.
2. **Repent:** Go to God first and cleanse your heart. Confess the things that are plaguing you. Confess the negative thoughts you are having. Confess your sins and ask God for forgiveness.
3. **Worship:** Worship the truth of who God is in your life. Worship His name and the mightiness of His name. Praise His name because of all you KNOW Him to be. Set your heart to one of awe, reverence, and praise

with God so that when you pray, you **know** He has the answers, He has the solutions, whether He gives them to you or **not**.

Prayers to Reference in the Bible	
Prayer	*Scripture*
The Lord's Prayer	*Matthew 6: 9 – 13*
Nehemiah's Prayer	*Nehemiah 9*
Hannah's Prayer	*1 Samuel 2*
King Hezekiah's Prayer	*2 Kings 19: 14-19*
David's Prayer	*1 Chronicles 29: 10-20*
Jesus's Prayer	*John 17*

6 A WALK THAT IS GUIDED

"Life offers many instructions along the way. We just rarely look up on our journey to see them."
~Jeanice Sherai

One of my favorite books of the Bible is the book of Psalms and one of my favorite stories in the Bible, is the story of King David.

Despite everything King David went through and encountered... he was still known as a man after God's own heart. He followed God's paths no matter what came His way. He stuck with God. King David wasn't a perfect man, just like us, but King David was a man that knew WHO to turn to in his imperfect ways.

The Book of Psalms was written in its majority by King David, but he quite possibly wasn't the only author of this book. Psalms 119 does not actually have an author listed or recorded for anyone to **truly** say who wrote it. It is believed that it is a Psalm of David while others say that Nehemiah or Ezra must have written it.

It's strange to me that the author is unknown for Psalms 119 because it is the *longest* chapter in the Bible and if I take my time to write anything that long, you best believe I am putting my name on it ☺. Who else agrees?

But seriously, Psalms 119 is probably my favorite chapter in the book of Psalms. It immediately starts off by teaching us about the way in which we should go.

The Message Bible translates Psalms 119:1 to say, "You're blessed when you stay on course, walking steadily on the road revealed by God."

I don't know about you, but that immediately grabs my attention. Suddenly I'm wondering, what is this path and am I truly on it? Am I following God's Word as I walk? Am I walking on the paths that He has paved?

There are **so** many questions that we tend to have concerning our journey. The truth is, a lot of the questions may remain unanswered because we are on a faith walk that God desires for His children to take.

Yes, we do read **many** stories where God gives **specific** directions to His children and He will also do the same for us at certain points in our life, but the truth is, even with those instructions, we still tend to mess up along the way. We tend to veer off His path, we tend to let fear lead us astray even though we **know** within that God has told and shown us the way He desires for us to go.

It seems to me that the Psalmist in Psalms 119 is depressed at the time of this writing, and I wonder if that is why he wrote this chapter but never truly signed his name. He seemed depressed, but still had hope in God's guidance. He seemed depressed, but still knew that God's way was His only way. He endured judgement and ridicule, but still made the decision that He would choose God's way.

> **Question to Consider:**
>
> When the world is coming against you and even when you are angry with God, do you tend to stay on His path or decide to take another route? Where have you ventured off God's path due to unforeseen circumstances?

"Thy WORD is a lamp unto my feet, and a light unto my path. "

Psalms 119: 105

Speak that aloud once. Go ahead, do it. ☺

It is one of the most **powerful** affirmations that you will **ever speak** over your life. Don't miss this chance.

It is also confirmation of a few things in our life:

1. God desires to **lead** us.
2. God has given us **access** to a Word that He promises will **lead** us.
3. God has a path that He desires for us to **follow**.

God made no mistakes in sharing how in even some of our darkest moments, His **Word** would be our **light**. His word would **lead** us on the paths that we should take.

Have you ever walked somewhere at night and there were no streetlights? How did you feel? Were you afraid? Did you have to use anything to light your path in order to see?

God's Word tells us in Psalms 119 that in those places in our life where it seems **so** dark that we cannot see which way to take that we must allow **His Word** to be our **light**.

Easier said than done right? Trust me, I know.

However, I will tell you that His Word and His way are a lot easier to follow than the darkness of this world. God's Word will bring peace to your life in the places where this world will almost always bring depression, anxiety, and chaos if we allow its darkness to lead.

My Personal Journey

My journey out of my comfort zone and into the unknown wasn't an easy journey. To be quite "Frank (even though my name is Jeanice Sherai ☺)," it was downright hard and very frustrating.

Sometimes, there was no visibility on my path, nor was there ever much light at all it seemed. Only enough light to direct my feet, but never enough light to illuminate the entire path before me. I wanted the sun to shine, and

God was handing me a flashlight to use to guide my feet.

I will never forget one day on a conference call at work. It was bright and early on a Monday morning and I was talking to this woman who had the absolute sweetest voice while we waited for others to join our meeting. I will call her Samantha for privacy sakes ☺.

Samantha and I dialed into this conference call where others were supposed to join as well. Well, it so happens on this day that no one else joined the call.

So, Samantha says to me, "You know Sherai, I read and I recite what I read a lot because I've been through some horrific times and those times caused me to lose my short-term memory." She continued, "I guess God just wanted to protect me because there are times and things that I just no longer remember."

(*trigger warning below)

She then begins to talk to me about enduring the loss of her child during their sleep. She then asked if could she read something to me.

I tell her yes, please go ahead and read.

She began to read this excerpt from a book titled, "The Dark Night of the Soul" written by Allison E. Peers and when she finishes reading the excerpt, she says to me,

"Sherai, I don't know why God chooses to take some of us down the darkest paths and to walk through some of the roughest times, but He does."

She goes on to share with me that everything in life can't be explained. This woman amid deep, unexplainable, and unbearable pain understood that in times that we don't understand what God is doing, God is still *doing* something. He is still working in our lives in ways that He knows is needed.

Samantha knew that what God was doing in her life, even if it drove her to despair, was always a part of His plan. She knew that the work God does in us, although we sometimes have no awareness of, is always a work that actually **needs** to be done.

Samantha confessed that at times on her journey, it felt like God was ripping her life completely apart, but in actuality, He was preparing her soul and spirit for a deeper level and a brand-new thing.

We talked even more deeply on that call that morning and she asked if she could pray to end the conference call. I immediately bought the book she read from even though it seemed so out of my level of understanding but at the same time so very intriguing. I read this book so slowly that even to this day, I am still reading it.

It made me wonder just how often God shows up on our path, but we don't recognize that it's Him? Here I was driving to work with tons of questions on my mind and He let me know immediately through divine timing that He indeed hears me.

I knew **instantly** that this divine arrangement and timing was God. I knew that even though I felt ignored, God was letting me know that He sees and hears me. He was letting me know that He understood that His daughter was tired and this strange work call, was His graceful and love-filled **nudge** along the way.

What if I had chosen instead to rush off this conference call with Samantha simply because I wanted that quiet time to myself as I drove?

I would have surely missed God's fresh manna and thirst-quenching water on a day that it was totally unexpected, but so deeply needed.

> **Question to Consider:**
>
> Where is God showing up and nudging you along, but you're refusing to look up and acknowledge Him because it's simply not the way you expected?

It's funny because we often cry out desperately that we **need** God's direction, but simultaneously reject it once we get it. Isn't that ironic?

We will pray and pray for God to show up and then when He does, we say," Nah, *that's not God."*

God is telling us what He wants us to do, but a lot of times, we choose to keep <u>running</u> from what He is saying.

> We pray and pray **so hard** for God to **show up**, to give us confirmation, but the reality is that even the ask for confirmation is a sign of a lack of faith. We end up being like Gideon (Judges 6:33-40) where what God uses to <u>show</u> us it's Him, we need to see again because once is never enough.
>
> **~Jeanice Sherai**

I truly believe God is a patient God, so He will **keep** speaking until we hear Him, and He will continuously use everything on our journey, even during our unbelief, for our good when we are called according to His purpose (Romans 8:28). I truly believe that nothing on our journey is wasted. That alone gives me rest in the midst of my journey of wondering if I have truly taken the wrong way. When my mind begins to make me question if I truly heard God correctly, that alone gives me rest on my journey.

I also believe God is All-Knowing. So even when He leads and guides us, He still knows which direction we will take **and** how long it will take for us to get to His **destined** place.

I believe that more than **anything** the truth, above all else, has been **one** of the most comforting things on my journey from worrying and being overly anxious concerning where I was currently, to where I was headed.

Yet, I must admit, although I was obedient concerning following God and stepping out on my journey... my behavior was *still* very similar to the Israelites (*deep sigh).

If you are not familiar with the story of the Israelites, Google will tell you in short form their entire story. The Bible will give you this story in detail, and I also have a devotional with my husband, entitled "31 Days of Faith: From Familiarity to Freedom" that will walk you through their journey in daily doses as well.

I encourage you to check out all three resources and really study the journey of the Israelites. I pray it gives you encouragement and discernment to know that we have all struggled to trust and follow God's way.

There were so many times that I would complain and complain, and ask question after question to God concerning my journey.

Honestly…. I still do it (*deep sigh).
I'm quicker to step out and be obedient these days, but I **know** that I *still* make God's eyes roll at me on a regular basis. I mean, the truth is, sometimes I'm truly sick of myself **and** my questions. So, I know He is LOL.

I remember once I went on this retreat that was so absolutely life changing. One of the activities was to choose one thing you would leave behind and not take forward with you on your journey.

I chose my **questions**. I have to be honest with you and tell you that right after I left that place, I stopped and picked up those same questions.

It's so hard to travel a journey with **only** the promise of God tucked in your pocket. No one else has heard this promise. No one else gets why you are taking this way. You are not even sure if **you** even heard it correctly, but yet you know that something mighty is within you tugging you to keep going in this way.

When you're on a journey and:
1. **The cost is higher to turn back rather than keep going,**
2. <u>**You**</u> **can't explain to others <u>how</u> you know that**

what's ahead is where God is calling you, but you know <u>within</u> that it is indeed Him, or
3. None of the things you are using to explain your sporadic behavior makes sense *even* to you, but yet and still something within you keep's shouting: keep going.

> **That's how you will <u>know</u> that it is God. We can never explain God's path, but we can trust Him to make it all make sense as we continue to follow Him.**

What God leads us to do a lot of times will not make sense.

> **"God is not trying to do the normal, He's trying to do the miraculous in our lives."**
> **~Jeanice Sherai**

A lot of times, we open the door to confusion and chaos when we refuse to walk in the direction God is leading us, we begin to listen to the opinions of people over God's directions, and we allow our minds to continuously circle around the same questions filled with doubt rather than faith.

I have said this repeatedly throughout this book, but it never hurts to remind you again, that this is indeed a **faith** walk.

> **The key thing to remember is that when it's God there is peace. When it's the enemy there will always be chaos and confusion.**

You will have to trust the voice **within that is** leading you and allow His voice and His written Word to lead you forward.

Remember that God will never lead you to do anything that will compromise His written Word. He will never ask you to step **outside** His will to **fulfill** His will.

> So, as you follow His voice, His written Word should be your ultimate guide. He may be doing a new thing, but that new thing will never be a compromise to what has already been written.
> **~Jeanice Sherai**

7 WHEN JESUS INTERRUPTS YOUR DAY

"Sometimes the interruption is the path."
~Jeanice Sherai

Imagine that you are sitting at home one day and you hear a knock at your door. You wonder who this could be because you are definitely not expecting anyone and you honestly don't even *feel* like having company. You reluctantly head to the door and as you peep out your peephole, you see **Jesus**!

You have heard about this Man named Jesus. He is a popular voice and influencer in this day, but you have been reluctant to follow His teachings. There have been times when you have even questioned some of the things that He has said. I mean, who is going to continue to love people who set out to continuously hurt you.

You just don't agree with a lot of things that He has been saying and spreading around this world, and so to see Him at your door is absolutely astounding to you.

*"Can I even trust this Man? Why is he here to see **me**?"*

Imagine that you recently recall praying to God about a particular situation (bring that specific situation to mind if you can) that you were *desperate* to receive an answer. You were just not sure which road to take or which route to choose in the situation.

You were just about to head out for a walk to see if possibly God would give you direction concerning the situation, but that was interrupted by this soft, but yet loud, knock at your door. You wonder, "How in the world did I hear such a soft knock so loud?"

When you open the door, Jesus begins speaking, "Hey! I was wondering if I could walk with you today?"

"How does this man even know what I am about to do? Has He been following me or spying on me? Has He been listening somehow to my thoughts and prayers? Who is He that He is aware of where I am headed and what I am about to do next?"

You are peering at this man interested, but also very afraid.
I mean, it is a day and age where you just **don't trust** people and although you've heard about all of His greatness, you *still* don't know if He can be trusted.

Yet, you hear a whisper within you, nudging you and repeatedly saying, *"Say, yes"* and so grudgingly, timidly, and fearfully, you do.

You begin this walk with Jesus, and He asks you about this dilemma that you are facing. You never told Him you had a dilemma and now He's prying a bit *too* deep! As He talks, you are silent because you are still at a place where you are truly not sure *who* He *is*.

Jesus tells you that there is a way that "seems" right to man, but in the end that way will lead to death (Proverbs 14:12).

You're thinking, *"Great, thanks Jesus, that has **truly** helped me with this decision (*deep sigh)."*

Yet, no matter how frustrated you are with His interruption in your day, something compels you to keep listening, and so you do.

He goes on to tell you that in life, we must always follow the path that God has instructed even if it does not make sense because if God is the Way, then He most definitely knows the Way to get us to the place that we are going.

He tells you that on this path it is important that we **never** lean on our own understanding but that we always trust God with all our heart in the way that He is leading (Proverbs 3:5-6).

He then turns to you, and He asks, "What is keeping you in this place?" Jesus asks you to identify the emotions and questions that are keeping you from deciding to move forward from this place.

(Take time in this moment to identify a place that you are stuck and the reasons or questions that are keeping you stuck in that place.)

You begin to pour out your heart concerning where you are struggling, and He turns and says, "Now are these questions and emotions based on the God who created the earth or are they based on your limited understanding?"

Suddenly you are baffled by His question. You may not know much about this man, but He seems to know and understand **everything** about you. Things that you **know** you have **never** mentioned.

"How does He know these things," you wonder, *"I've never voiced them to anyone, honestly no one even **knows** about this dilemma."*

Jesus comforts you in this place. He lets you know that God is always with you, that He hears you, and that He **loves** to walk with you and instruct you along the way. Then, He says the catch is...we must **trust** the way God is instructing us over *our* way.

By this time, you are no longer skeptical, you **know** who this is, and you are listening earnestly as He speaks. The more you walk with Him, the more you understand the decision that you need to make. It just doesn't make sense to you to take *this* way.

You are thankful for this day, this walk, and the decision you made to walk with Jesus.

Understanding that God's ways and thoughts will **never** be like ours and will always be much higher than ours will always be **key** on our journey (Isaiah 55: 8 -9).

Go on a Walk with God

Set aside some time today to take a walk with God **alone**:
1. Just you,
2. God,
3. and your phone for research and safety precautions.

Talk to God about a major decision you are facing and how you are feeling about that decision.

As you share with Him the many different things you are

facing concerning this decision, keep a tab of the emotions, the feelings, and the questions that you have as you talk with Him.

Make a note of the things that stick out in your spirit as you walk and talk with God.

As you walk:
1. Search for a quiet place and pause.
2. Begin to observe the way you felt as you talked to God about this decision.
3. What if any of those emotions and feelings came from God?
4. Take time to search God's word for scriptures that speak to how you are currently feeling.
5. Ask and allow God to lead you to scriptures He wants to use to speak to you about this decision.
6. Make a note of the scriptures in your phone.
7. Continue on your walk.

As you resume your walk with God, begin to discuss this same decision with God. Use the scriptures He gave you to begin speaking to the places where you are inserting your feelings, emotions, questions, and concerns. Let His Word be the tool that is used to instruct you on the direction you should take in this situation.

Once you are back home, take time to journal about what God revealed to you **and** the decision that you will make. Be confident in your decision. God promises to never leave you nor forsake you (Deuteronomy 31:6).

Believe His word!

_____
_____
_____
_____
_____
_____
_____
_____
_____
_____

Equipping You on Your Walk with God

HOW DOES THE HOLY SPIRIT INSTRUCT US IN OUR WALK WITH GOD?

1. **Allow the Holy Spirit to guide your research.**
   a) Read Psalms 119 in its entirety.
   b) Study the way that God has led others throughout

the Bible.
- c) Google scriptures related to following God.
- d) Talk to your pastor and other wise counsels around you.
- e) Ask questions as you continue to go deeper.
- f) Ask God to continuously reveal more to you concerning your journey.
2. **Reminder: If your heart is not in the right place, address your heart issues FIRST** (i.e., if you are seeking God concerning a situation, but you already have rules and limitations about "what you not gone do (*side-eye)," then clear that up first!). God can give you clarity in that place so that you can be free from those limitations and are able to **hear** Him clearly.
3. **Once your heart is in the right place...PRAY and seek Him for guidance.**

HOW TO ENSURE YOUR HEART IS IN THE RIGHT PLACE (THIS WILL BE REPEATED THROUGHOUT THIS BOOK)

1. **Fast:** The Bible shows us so many examples of individuals who gathered in groups to fast or who simply fasted individually to **truly** hear from God concerning a situation. Fasting is when we make physical sacrifices in order to spiritually grow closer with God. Fasting removes distractions so that you can develop a more intimate relationship with God and recognize who He is in your life.
2. **Repent:** Go to God first and cleanse your heart.

Confess the things that are plaguing you. Confess the negative thoughts you are having. Confess your sins and ask God for forgiveness.

3. **Worship:** Worship the truth of who God is in your life. Worship His name and the mightiness of His name. Praise His name because of all you KNOW Him to be. Set your heart in one of awe, reverence, and praise with God so that when you pray, you **know** He has the answers and that He has the solutions, whether He gives them to you or **not**.

> There is a journey in life that God wants to take us on. A lot of times, we are waiting for God to tell us more, but God is waiting for us to do something with the instructions He has already provided.
>
> **~Jeanice Sherai**

Reference of People who Walked with God in the Bible	
Individual	*Scripture*
Abraham	Genesis 11
David	1 Samuel 16
Nehemiah	Nehemiah
Noah	Genesis 5
John the Baptist	Luke 3

8 I DON'T KNOW WHERE TO GO

"Even when a walk is guided, we can sometimes STILL end up lost."

~Jeanice Sherai

I get it. I know that we often understand that God will guide our walk, but I also get that even when He guides us, we *still* struggle to know the **way**.

There are times when God speaks to us, and He tells us **clearly** where to go and what to do. Yet, we still sit still wondering if that is the direction we should take or if we heard God correctly even though He has confirmed it a thousand times. We allow our minds to fill with all the things that could go wrong if we take this direction.

> We forget that if God instructed us to take this route, then He too has taken it as well. His Word promises that He has already gone before us on our journey.
> **~Jeanice Sherai**

Can you relate? Have you ever received the **clearest** directions from God and still not understood where to go from there? I know I have, and I **still** can struggle with receiving what God has spoken concerning my journey. I still can struggle with allowing those instructions to be planted deep within with the water of faith.

I tend to take what God has spoken to me and then over-analyze it completely.

"What exactly did He mean? Did He mean leave that behind when He said ALL things? Did He mean stop doing

that work when He told me to rest, did He?"

It is not that I don't trust God, it is that I rarely ever trust **me**. Lately, I have had to remind myself repeatedly that I **have** the mind of Christ (1 Corinthians 2:16).

I remind myself of this so that I can always be sure of the promise that it is Christ who lives in me and greater is He that is in me, than he that is in this world (1 John 4:4). I need to know that God is BIG and if His BIGNESS resides in **me**, then I am **unstoppable** in this world. Who else needed that reminder today?

I can tell you honestly that I do not appear to trust that I have the **mind** of Christ when it is time for me to take the biggest steps that God has instructed me to take. It is almost like I forget that the God who led me before is the *same* God who is leading me now.

The very essence of me allowing fear to keep me stuck externally because I was not sure if this BIG God that I served could *truly* be trusted is the internal battle that I fight daily.

That is such a hard truth to admit. At times, I have sat on God's instructions because I did not believe His Word enough to trust that the mind that He had given me could and actually did hear Him correctly. This in turn meant that I honestly also was struggling with my belief in the things I had read and studied concerning the very One who sent His own Son to save me.

How could I trust Him to be my Savior, but not trust His direction?

There have been *so* many times that I've sat at the feet of Jesus, received all of His promises and truth, but then get up from that place and allow the worries of this world to quickly snatch everything God had taught me away.

After doubt kicked in, I did not trust the plan or the instruction I had received, and I was back at Jesus' feet again asking Him the same questions.

"Are you sure God? Help me to know where to go from here!"

I know that God is not a God of confusion, but somehow, even after being at the feet of Jesus, receiving confirmation not only just within but also externally, I could still allow seeds of doubt, worry, and confusion to enter my mind and confuse me.

Do you know what confusion does to our mind? It keeps us going in circles around a thing. Prime example...the Israelites circled their mountain in the wilderness for 40 years not moving forward into their destiny due to confusion (Deuteronomy 2:3).

We can have the ***clearest*** of instructions and still choose to not move forward into the path that will lead us to the places God has called us, prepared us, purposed us, and destined for us to be. Then, as we stand or sit there stagnant, we decide to go back to God to confirm once more that it is indeed Him leading us.

We go back to Jesus' feet, begging God for more direction, when we have yet to follow the last set of instructions that He gave us.

Due to our lack of faith, we decide to stop moving if we do not know where each step on our path will take us. Have you ever been there? Are you there now? Has God ever given you direction and you *still* were filled with so many different questions? Did you stand still or did you keep moving?

"They won't accept me there."
"Everyone will laugh at me."
"What will people think?"
"I'm not good enough."
"I don't have what it takes."
"I can't afford to take that route."

Have you ever thought that once you take one step towards where God is leading, He will meet you right there in that place and lead you on to the next step? We will never know what is next unless we get the courage to walk in the way that God is leading.

Here is my tip: Just begin.

Abraham was a man who followed the leading of God. Abraham was given instructions by God, but the instructions He received did not provide all the answers that he needed.

> ***Now the LORD said to Abram, "Go from your country and your kindred and your father's house to the land that I will show you.***
> ***Genesis 12:1***

If you notice, God did not say, *"I need you to go up the street, turn left, stop by Aunt Mabel's house, leave out of there in 29 minutes, then go to the 7-11 across the street, there you will find a brown piece of paper giving you more instructions."*

No, God told Abraham that He had to leave to go in the direction He was calling and the only other piece of information He provided in that verse is the promise that He would show Abraham this land. God went on to tell Abraham, that He would bless his life for following His way by going to this place that He would show him. Do you know what Abraham did? He went in the direction that God instructed him to go.

> ***So, Abram went, as the LORD had told him; and Lot went with him. Abram was seventy-five years old when he set out from Harran.***
> ***Genesis 12:4***

We don't truly know the ridicule Abraham received from family and friends as he took this route. We don't know if people tried to hold him back and keep him from going, but what we do know is that he **went** and there were a few loyal people who decided to go with him.

Your journey to where God is taking you will require a whole lot of **faith** and a whole lot of **leaving**. In order to go in the direction that God would have you to go, you will have to leave your questions, your worries, your concerns, and sometimes *your very own people* behind.

A lot of times, it is not that we don't know where to go, it is that we are not sure if it is God **leading,** which can be the true struggle in knowing when it is God: Having the courage to believe that it is truly *Him.*

> **Where God leads, He confirms.**

As you take steps on your path, you will know it is God because He will continuously confirm His way. It may not always be in the most *obvious* ways, but He always shows up to nudge us along and ***usually*** it is when we are just about ready to give up and head back in the other direction. Trust that the God who leads, also confirms where He leads.

A Letter to A Strong Soul on a Beautiful Journey

This chapter is not as long as others because it is a journaling chapter. I want you to truly take time to first pray to God for direction (there goes that word again). Do not question what you believe is being spoken into your heart. Trust the God who spoke it. Once you hear from God, I want you to begin writing to yourself the words that God has spoken. This is a Holy Spirit led letter. This letter is not self-led, and I do not want you to believe for one moment that it is. Absolutely nothing is by coincidence. The words you are beginning to write will be filled with encouragement, beauty, and direction concerning your journey and are prophetic. Hold them in your heart once they are written, envision them when the letter is complete, and walk your life path with this letter and the promise of God as your company.

Hey! Do not skip this part of the book! Do not take this lightly! Get to writing 😊!

_____

_____

_____

_____

HOW DO YOU KNOW WHEN IT'S GOD?

JEANICE SHERAI DURRAH

_____

_____

_____

_____

_____

_____

Let me tell you that you are absolutely beautiful! You are fearfully and wonderfully made! You may think that this one step means nothing, but to God...it means everything. I pray you see just how directed your paths are and how much God cares about the tiniest details of your life. There have been many places I have entered in life that I would think were coincidence. None of them were, they all made a difference, they all nudged me further on my path.

> I have to tell you that everyone won't agree with every stop on your path, but your job is to be in agreement with God, not people.
> **~Jeanice Sherai**

9 MEDITATE ON GOD'S WORD DAY AND NIGHT

"It will be very hard to know when God is speaking to me, if I refuse to listen to His voice speaking in His very own Word."

~Jeanice Sherai

We are quite a **different** generation than the ones that came before us.

It is so hard to convince my generation and the ones following of truth, *even* when we are given a book that we are told is **filled** with it. I'm not sure why, but in this generation and the ones following, God made us hard hearted and stubborn in many ways. I wonder sometimes if it is to cause His followers to dig deeper and discover a truth that has always been there, but many generations before were too filled with tradition and religion to discover or experience it.

Yet, let me scale back and acknowledge that I believe that the generations before us were created in the way that they were in order to prepare for a generation like **us**. I believe those generations have purpose just like my generation and future generations do as well.

I truly believe the older generations were created with hearts that would be steadfast in God's truth so that they can continuously guide and point us in His way, but that does not mean my generation or the generations that come after me will easily follow, and I believe that God knew just that when He created us.

He knew the questions we would have, the journey we would take to get to Him, and the times we would turn away.

Peter just **knew** he was in a place where he would not turn from God. He just **knew** that his walk was *so* far along, that he was so deep in God's Word, that he had seen **enough** of God that he would **never** turn his back on the One who showed up in his life and not only blessed him and saved him, but also changed the trajectory of his life.

> ***Jesus answered, "I tell you, Peter, before the rooster crows today,*** *you will deny three times* ***that you know me."***
> *Luke 22:34*

I wonder if Peter was angry with God for not believing his word that he would not betray Him. I mean, we know that God knows our every step, but I wonder if Peter was still mad as he went on his way absolutely determined **not** to betray God and determined to show *Him*.

You see, we can be adamant in our journey on the ways we will take, we can be adamant on the decisions we will *not* make, **but God** knows the real story. The good news is that God wrote those steps into our story as well. He created our very being and in creating us, He knows the intricacies of us. He ***knows*** what we will do.

Jesus knew Peter better than Peter knew himself and when Jesus rose again, like He said He would, He wanted Peter to know first that He was **still** his friend.

"But go, tell his disciples and Peter that he is going before you to Galilee. There you will see him, just as he told you."
Mark 16:7

God understands our hearts. He knows that we won't always have hearts that are easily softened to His Word and to His instructions. Yet, God still makes a daily/hourly/minute by minute decision to love us and **show** us His way.

> **I must tell you that one of the biggest ways to know when it's God, is to know His voice and how He has spoken to others through His Word.**

I know, I know, some of you are now ready to be done with this book but give it a chance for a second and just keep reading. This is not to convince you of anything. The Word speaks for itself. There is no convincing needed.

I actually think that many people battle with the truth of God's Word because deep within them, their souls know it is true, but their mind and flesh want to convince them of something entirely different.

We would rather be comfortable in a lie rather than be uncomfortable in the truth in order to grow in our relationship with God. We would rather not face ourselves and remain in the dark than receive the beauty of God's **light**.

I am not telling you to go and read the Bible, but if you *are* reading this book, then you *are* in this moment curious as to *how* you will know when it's God.

> **Here is one of the key ways that you will know: His instruction will align with His Word.**

If you have not put this book down yet 😊, let me share with you my story of how I began to **know** when it was God.

My Personal Journey

I have always been a person who journaled, wrote poetry (not as often anymore), and read tons and tons of books. Growing up I would literally spend most of my hours in my room reading books or writing. If I was not in my room reading, I was at the kitchen table reading, I was sitting in the den or in the bedroom with my parents, *reading.* I loved to read, and my parents never took this love away from me. They allowed me to continuously read honestly whatever I could get my hands on.

Well, I'm convinced that God planted this desire within me. I am also convinced that he used my love to read and developed a hunger within me to know more about Him through reading His Word. He knew that one day my love for reading and writing would transform into a longing to read His Word and journal what I believed He was speaking specifically to me.

I would say around 2007, I began to wake up every single morning to read God's Word and journal about the scriptures I was reading. I mean, I could have gone to the club the night before, stayed out to 4am and I would **still** wake up that morning anxious and hungry to dive even deeper into God's Word.

There was not a morning where I wasn't before God, reading His Word and journaling about what it spoke to me. I filled journal after journal after journal of what I believed God's Word was speaking.

Now, some of these journals I ripped up and tossed out in anger because I realized that along my journey a lot of the things, I thought God was speaking, I had truly gotten **wrong**. I was angry that my desires did not happen, but God's will did. I was angry that God never bent or compromised His Word to satisfy me. I was humiliated that I was wrong. How could I spend all this time with God and still get life wrong?

> If you are being led to do something that compromises the very essence, character, and fruit of who God is…. that is not God.
> **~Jeanice Sherai**

I know, **trust me I know**. That one truth can suck tremendously, but God **will never change**. He is the same yesterday, today, and forever. He is not going to change to fit our desires or needs. There were *so* many times that I thought God was leading me in ways that **completely** went against every single thing written in His Word (*deep sigh).

Y'all there will still be many *other* times where I will get it wrong, but now I know that His Word is a true reference and map for me. That does not mean that even in writing this book, I will always get it right, but what it does mean is that every time I do not get it right, I am learning even more about who God is, how He speaks, and how He leads, and His Word is always there for me to meditate on and reference.

Life is a journey and the destination is Eternity.

We cannot give up in our quest to know **when** it's God. We must choose to let go of pride and grab hold of Him because when we surrender self, He will show up and show us *so* many things.

God will lead us to do many things that are not traditional, that are out of the box, that won't fit what those around us believe we should be doing, but it **will fit His Word**.

Trust me, it is <u>never</u> fun to be out of the will of God or to be disobedient to His Word. There is **no** peace in that place. There is **no** joy in that place. However, I will tell you what *is* present in that place.... confusion, heartache, strife, jealousy, and every other fruit of darkness. The fruit of light is *so* tasty, that I just hope as you read this chapter, *even* if you are forcing yourself to do it 😊, that you gain an appetite to try His fruit for yourself.

> **Question to Consider:**
>
> **Where are you struggling to know if it's God, but also dealing with a conscience that is repeatedly warning you that none of the fruit of that situation matches the character of God and His Word?**

Why would God put us in things that would cause us confusion, heartache, strife, and destruction? A lot of times, we use God's Word when we want to and we toss it out when it does not agree with us. I remember many times I justified staying in a toxic relationship or around a toxic friend because love is patient and kind (1 Corinthians 13 *side-eye*). **Yet**, I could not use God's Word to sit down that habit or stop doing that thing that I knew was causing me to be divided within. When I wanted it to work for my good, I would allow it, when I did not, I would come up with every excuse as to how it was justified, "His grace is sufficient right (*deep sigh*)"?

Y'all I am still **in** my walk, I am **still** fighting my flesh and I do not always win. **Actually,** a lot of times I lose, but I **still** wake up to fight again.

God's Word is a good measure for everything.

How do we know when it's God?

Pay Attention.

Pay attention to how He speaks in the Bible.
Pay attention to how He instructs.
Pay attention to when He commanded people to obey.
Pay attention to when He gave them permission to go against the grain.
Pay attention to how **He speaks** because He is **still** speaking in the same way.

It may not be the same instructions, but He's using the same voice and God has not and will not ever change. As we read God's Word we must not lean on our own understanding (Proverbs 3:5) instead we must let His Holy Spirit lead us concerning what God is speaking to **us** specifically in that scripture.

The Word does not change, but He could be speaking to you concerning a specific situation and it could be loud and clear what He is saying. Yet, another time you can go back and read the **same** scripture and God can allow His Holy Spirit to speak to your heart this time using that same scripture in a **completely** different way.

> **How will you know when it's God? Meditate. Meditate on His Word, day and night.**

God says we are to meditate on His Word, day and night and if you don't know by now, I am a **big** proponent of meditation. Meditation has been one thing that God has taught me as He has led me into an even deeper relationship with Him. He started me with journaling and reading His Word (which I still wake up and do every single morning), but then He taught me to go deeper. He taught me how to meditate with Him on the Word that He is speaking. It is in those moments of chewing and meditating on His Word, that my heart has gained the **fullest** of understanding.

Many say that they cannot meditate, and I just say to them that we do not yet understand what meditation is and how to meditate. My meditation practice could be very different from yours. The way you meditate could be simply repeating God's Word over and over in your mind as you drive to work allowing the Holy Spirit to give you understanding as you ponder each portion of that verse. You could also take a walk and meditate on a verse you read this morning as you walk, talking to Jesus about what He is speaking to you in that verse. This is one of my favorite ways to meditate.

Another way I meditate is in a still, small space. It is with slow, steady breathing where I am literally inhaling and exhaling God's Word over my life. My focus is completely on His Word. Usually, I choose one verse to meditate on and I choose one word from that verse that speaks to me entirely. As I ponder that verse, I ponder that word and what God is speaking to me that day. It is through meditation that I have grown to know a God that is completely loving, completely filled with peace, and brings complete understanding to the trials, worries, and storms of my day.

When I meditate on God's Word concerning a situation, I hear God in the **clearest** way. It is in that moment that I truly **know** that it is God. A lot of times meditation may not bring me answers, but it does bring me peace. I get up from that place knowing that as much as I'm concerned with the issues of my life, God is **not**. He has those under control, even when my mind is running rampant and wanting me to believe otherwise.

> **Question to Consider:**
>
> Do you just read God's Word and keep moving or do you sit and truly ponder and study what He is saying?

We cannot just read God's Word and not dig deeper. Sometimes it is very relevant that we understand the times and the audience that is being spoken to in scripture. If not, we will be angry and confused wondering why God would speak or command such a thing. We must understand the times that these people were being spoken to and what they were dealing with on a daily basis. Then you will know that the way God lead them was the **best** way for them in the times that they were living.

In that same way, you will gain an understanding that God can see into your situation and He knows the best way to lead you in the place you are in. His instructions for you may not be like His instructions for others. Many people in the Bible experienced God leading them in a way that was completely different from how others were led, but they followed Him anyway.

Noah was led to build an ark and no one believed him. Guess what he did? He built an ark anyway. There he was building an ark in preparation for a flood and there was literally no sight of rain.

> "God will instruct you to protect you and an entire generation, but it is up to you to believe His Word and follow His way."
> **~Jeanice Sherai**

If we do not know God's Word, we will not recognize His voice and it is just that simple. I did not start off knowing when God was speaking to me, I had to develop a relationship with Him first.

> "Your relationship with God will determine how well and how clearly you recognize and hear His voice."
> **~Jeanice Sherai**

The way I developed a relationship with God was by spending time with Him, being honest with Him, and getting to know who He was, is, and will always be to me personally. I knew that my parent's relationship with God could not save me. I had to know who He was intimately for myself.

I would sit with my Bible, my journal, and my coffee and I would ask God honest questions. I would tell Him everything and literally be **very** honest with Him about what I was thinking and feeling. I continue to do this **daily**. As much as I talk, I also listen. I am *still* learning who God is through His Word, through His chosen vessels, and through how He works in my life.

> Developing a relationship with God, spending time with Him, talking to Him, and praying to Him will always be key in knowing when it's God.

Think about it. How can you be friends with a person if you don't *truly* know them? How can you be in a relationship with a boyfriend/girlfriend if you never take time to get to know them?

It's not possible. The same goes for God.

Your relationship with God will not be based on perfection or getting it right, it will be based on His love and His promises to keep perfecting in you what **He started**. It is **God** working in us to do His will and He knows the work it will take to get us to the place that He needs us.

> Do you truly want to know when it's God? Develop a personal relationship with Him just as you would a new friend in your life. Study His Word to understand His character, pay attention to how He speaks. This is how you will know when it's God.

Meditate

Find A Quiet Place.
Find a Scripture on a topic that you are struggling with today.
Read that Scripture 3 times aloud.
What word speaks to you?
Focus on that word.
Begin to pay attention to your breath (Inhale & Exhale).
Pray silently: Ask God to use that word to speak to you.
Listen.
Note: Do not worry about thoughts that come and go, focus on the word before you and the scripture you chose.

10 A COFFEE DATE WITH JESUS

"There is nothing like a hot cup of coffee and a conversation with Jesus."
~Jeanice Sherai

Imagine getting a text from Jesus on your phone:

Incoming Text: "Meet me at 7?"
Your Response: "Okay."
Incoming Text: "See you at the coffee shop by your home."
Your Response: "I will be there."

You place your phone back down and you begin to immediately wonder what this meeting could be about.

"What could Jesus possibly want with me?"
"Is it because I didn't pay my tithes last week? "
"Is it because I cussed Richard out the other day?"
"Is it because I didn't put the buggy in the designated place?"

All of these questions begin to fill your mind. You cannot understand what you could have done that was *so* wrong that Jesus wants to actually meet with you in person.

Your mind is running rampant, but there is also an excitement bubbling within you as you get ready to go and meet *HIM* at the coffee shop.

You arrive at the coffee shop 15 minutes early because you know... "Jesus is always on time (**side-eye*)" and you do not want to add another thing to His list to speak to you about today.

Already in your mind, you are ready to confess and repent to Him about all that you can remember that you have done and then ask for forgiveness for the things you literally cannot remember. You want to make things right with Jesus and if He is meeting you person, you believe you have done something *very* wrong.

You look around the shop for the perfect table.

The barista welcomes you and asks you if you are ready to place your order and you tell her you will wait. Suddenly, you can feel a shift in the atmosphere. It is almost like a wind just blew through the shop, but there are no windows open and it is a hot and humid summer day.

You look up and there He is. Jesus arrives at 7:00 pm on the dot and He is walking towards your table.

To your shock, He has two filled coffee mugs in His hand.

"I ordered your favorite," Jesus says as He sits down at the table. You begin to wonder how He *even* knows your favorite.

"I know everything about you," Jesus replies.

"Did I ask that question aloud?"

You did not think you said it aloud, but then again, this is Jesus, He knows my thoughts.

You sit staring in awe at the Man before you. There is a peace over you that is unexplainable. All your fears and all your worries have suddenly disappeared.

Your anxiety is even no longer present.

"Who is this Man, that completely brings me peace, simply by being in His presence," you wonder within.

"**I AM**," Jesus replies.

You stare at Him in confusion as He sits staring directly into your eyes. You want to talk, but you would rather sit and listen.

Jesus begins speaking to you as He grabs your hands. "I've been wanting to get to know you. Yes I created you, but I want a relationship with my daughter. I want to hear your voice in the mornings. I want to speak with you throughout your day. I want to comfort you in your deepest troubled times. I want to rejoice with you in the midst of the biggest joys of your day."

"I want time with you. I want to experience your life **with** you. I want to be your friend, your comforter, your counselor, your protector, and your provider. I desire to be everything that you could possibly think to need."

You listen and you honestly feel slightly ashamed.

You begin to wonder, *"Have I truly avoided Jesus?"* You suddenly realize that although you *do* acknowledge Him as your Savior and you do pray, you rarely ever take time to *truly* spend with Him.

Life had happened and, in its happenings, it has engrossed you to the point where you were simply just trying to make it. Yet, suddenly you realized, *"How could I ever make it if I don't include Jesus."*

So, you begin to open up and share and Jesus...begins to listen.
....

What would you share with Jesus on this coffee date?
What would you ask Him?
What would you confess?

Sit for a moment and think about this coffee date as if it was truly a real date.

If you are a coffee drinker, grab your coffee.
Have a date with Jesus today.

Then write about your experience.

_____

_____

HOW DO YOU KNOW WHEN IT'S GOD?

Have you ever had someone tell you something that a friend did, and you responded with conviction, "I know my friend, they would *never* do what you are describing?"

What would happen if you got to know Jesus in that same way?

Take time to write about it. How can you strengthen your current relationship with Jesus?

_____

_____

_____

_____

_____

_____

_____

_____

_____

HOW DO YOU KNOW WHEN IT'S GOD?

> "I can tell you that what we a lot of times fear concerning having a relationship with Jesus, is a tactic of the enemy. Our greatest life begins when we begin a relationship with the One who created our very being."
> **~Jeanice Sherai**

11 A GOD WHO IS ALWAYS SPEAKING

"If you want to hear God, pay attention."
~Jeanice Sherai

One thing that my spiritual mentor, Mrs. Barbara has often spoken to me is that "God is always speaking." I am so glad that she has never been able to see my *many* eye-rolls when this has been her response to me.

I have wanted to respond so many times, *"Then why can't I hear Him."* The truth of the matter is, I could not hear God because I was not listening (*deep sigh).

> "We truly just want His approval concerning what we are praying, we **rarely** want His truth."
> **~Jeanice Sherai**

The reality is, sometimes we do not want to hear God, even though we pray with all of our might to hear Him.

> "When our mind is running rampant, when we have our own agenda, when self is in the way, it is hard to hear the truth of God."
> **~Jeanice Sherai**

God is able to speak through anything.

God has spoken to me in the most peculiar ways. He has also spoken to individuals in the Bible in some of the strangest ways, but that is God. How He moves in our life can never be placed in a box. He uses the smallest things to get our attention because He knows what it will take for us to finally listen.

I know I have said this a few times throughout this book, but I truly believe in order to hear God and believe Him when He is speaking, we have to know Him and have a personal relationship with Him so that we can recognize His voice.

I consider absolutely nothing a coincidence, so when I pray and something *"different"* happens, **I know that it is God**. I often say that God has a sense of humor and trust me He does. There are times when God will ***repeatedly*** let me know He is leading me in a certain way. For instance, I can watch a movie, check social media, talk to a friend, or listen to a sermon and they will all be speaking on the very same thing.

I usually in those moments, giggle to myself, while looking up at Him saying, *"Okay God, I get it."*

I want to take you through a few different ways that God speaks. The ways in this chapter are not ALL of the ways that God speaks, but they are some of the ways that I've heard Him and read about Him and His voice.

God Speaks in the Silence

There are so many times when I have been crying out to God and I have heard absolutely nothing. I would be so frustrated and angry with God. I could not understand how He could see His daughter suffering and not answer or help her in her present situation. Looking back on those times now, I know His silence **was** my help.

Job experienced God's silence in the Bible. You see, God allowed the enemy to attack Job for no apparent reason. The enemy was roaming to and fro on the earth and God said, "Have you considered my servant, Job (Job 1:8)."

I would like to pause here for a moment and say, "Jesus, please consider allowing the enemy to consider *anyone* else **but** me in this season 😊."

No seriously, God tested Job and it was not an easy test. The outcome that we like to celebrate was Job receiving a double portion of everything, but the journey for Job to receive this portion was almost unbearably hard to face.

Not *only* that, but in the midst of Job's tragedy and suffering, it seemed that God was **silent**.

For a while, Job was okay. He told his friends, *"Though He slay me, yet I will trust Him (Job 13:15)."* What a mighty faith to have in the midst of unexplainable loss and sickness. Yet, it seems as we continue in Job's story that eventually he does get mad. Maybe he has become irritated by his friends. Maybe their consoling and trying to reason what God was doing had frustrated him to no end. Maybe, that is what led him to also question God. Maybe it was the length of the suffering with no answer.

The Bible does not really say how long Job went through these trials, but we do know that for a while, God was silent, but then He **answered** (Job 38: 1-18).

God let Job know that He **is** the Creator of **<u>this</u>** world, He formed the seas, He created the wind, and that He created Job, **Himself**. So as a God who created everything, can't we trust Him even in the places that bring us to our knees? Doesn't He know how each of our life experiences should go?

This answer from God, silenced Job but also brought Job to a much deeper understanding of who God is in his life. Job was humbled by God's response, and He repented for his questions and anger and began to pray a much more sincere prayer.

When God is silent with us, He's still speaking to us.

We just have to understand what exactly He is speaking even in the silence. Sometimes God is teaching us. Sometimes He is wanting us to walk through that place with the lessons we have learned from previous situations and actually apply them. This of course is not always easy. Most times we never do as well as we *think* we will on the tests given to us by God.

That is *still* okay. Most times, in the midst of God's tests we rarely recognize that it *is* actually a test; it is not until we look back that we *truly* recognize it. I am hoping that our glance back in recognition actually prepares us more efficiently for the next test because there will be a **next**.

When God is silent with us, sometimes it is because He has already spoken His answer and our continued questions and prayers to Him are due to a lack of faith and trust.

Judah knows **all** about the wait of God's deliverance in the midst of His silence. In this case, God was silent due to their lack of faith in what He had already promised. In Isaiah 30, the prophet Isaiah prophesies judgment and redemption against Judah. Judah had sought God for His truth, but when He spoke His truth, they did not want it. They were being attacked by the Assyrians and after witnessing Israel being conquered and carried into exile, they feared for their lives instead of trusting what God had spoken.

God promised Judah He would protect them, but they trusted Egypt's protection and power over an all-powerful God.

Since Judah did not trust God's protection and relied on Egypt's instead, God relinquished them to the Assyrians. He had Isaiah prophesy judgment over their lives by using the very things they thought they could trust for protection. Whew! Does that sound familiar?

We many times hold on to so many physical things that

we believe are our protection. Yet, our only protection on this earth is our All Powerful, Never Changing, Promise Keeping God.

Yet, Judah could still look at their mess and see God's faithfulness, just as we can too.

God is so faithful that even when His children mess up, He has a plan for redemption and restoration. God promised Judah that after a time of waiting, He would hear their cries and restore their lives and give them an ear to hear Him.

> "Sometimes the silence, is to build your trust in an uncomfortable place, so that when you leave that place, you will have learned to truly trust His voice and His guidance."
> **~Jeanice Sherai**

God speaks through Nature

I am a lover of all things in nature, well except snakes and bears and spiders. So, I guess, not *all* things, but let me just say the creation of nature by God is absolutely beautiful. I may not like all the creatures that reside in nature, but I do love the very being of nature.

There, is that better? I feel better at least. 😊

I often take silent walks through nature. I pay attention to the trees, the plants, the birds, the sky, and the creeks. I think about how creative of a God that we serve to think to put so much beauty on this earth. In those walks through nature, in those beautiful things, God often speaks to me.

Before you give me a side-eye, did you know that in Exodus 3, God spoke to Moses in the very same way? Moses received a call on his life through a burning bush. If He spoke to Moses through nature, is it not possible for Him to also speak to us in the same ways? We struggle to listen when the message does not come in the ways we pictured that it would.

I believe that nature is one of the most magnificent ways that God does speak. There have been so many times that I have walked in nature and something rare happens. I see an animal that is normally hidden in the day or something growing out of the ground in the most peculiar of places. In those moments, I pay attention. I ask myself, "is God speaking and if so, what is He speaking?" Then, I listen.

There is a voice within each of us, that will lead us to wisdom. It is not a loud voice. This voice is still and often small, but if you pay attention, it will give you peace, comfort, and sometimes answers concerning every single thing you are experiencing. I tune into this voice often. This voice is one of the greatest things that I am thankful for as I walk through earth. It is truly my helper.

I call this voice, The Holy Spirit.

Jesus actually promised us that this voice would be a helper for us (John 14:16). I can attest to you that in every single thing that I have ever faced, this voice within, has been **all** that I have needed.

Even in nature, the Holy Spirit can make plain what God is speaking.

We do not often hear this loud, audible voice, and I honestly never have. Yet, within me I have had a knowing, a confirmation that this indeed was God. This knowing came with a peace that was confirmation that I could trust what God was speaking within.

God tells us that we have the mind of Christ. If we have the mind of Christ, we can trust what He is truly revealing within.

We can know what God is speaking through the peace that He brings within or the struggle or chaos that we may feel.

When it flows, just like the streams of nature, it is God.

When it is forced, when there is tugging, when there is condemnation, it is not God. He does not want you apart of those things.

I want to remind you again to make sure to read about the Fruits of the Spirit in Galatians. When God speaks, it is those things that you will feel within. You will know that you can trust His Holy Spirit.

Journal Activity

Walk through nature this week. Walk silently. Begin your walk with no expectations except to be present with God. Bring your book with you and take time to listen. Take time to write down every single thing impressed upon you concerning the nature around you. Do not question, just write. We do not learn God's voice through always getting it right. We learn God's voice by trusting ourselves enough to know we hear Him and having the humility to know even in hearing Him we will not always understand exactly what He is speaking. Paul teaches us that we know in part (1 Corinthians 13: 9). So, if we only know in part, it may take some time for God to truly reveal to us everything He means when He is speaking.

Take time to learn how God speaks and what He is speaking through practice.

Write about it below:

_____

_____

HOW DO YOU KNOW WHEN IT'S GOD?

_____

_____

_____

_____

_____

_____

_____

Now, pray and ponder over what God spoke to you. Let His Holy Spirit lead you into all understanding concerning your experience with God.

God speaks through our circumstances

There have been so many times that I have prayed to God concerning a situation, a relationship, and friendship and literally the truth was **right** in front of me. The truth is, I was praying to God, *hoping* that He would change that **truth**. We tend to put our hope in the physical rather than trusting what God has already spoken and shown us in the spiritual. We know within us when it is **not** God, we just do not want to believe Him.

I can tell you that God will not change His mind, but He does give us free will, and even when we take the route that's not His best, He will love us still. How many of us have taken a route when we felt God tugging us within saying that is not the right way? **I know I have.**

Somehow, I would find it in me to interpret a few verses in the Bible to justify that this *is* the way. I could be in the wrong relationship and justify it by saying, well God's Word does say that "love is patient and kind." I would rationalize it all by saying to myself, "maybe I am just not being patient enough." I could be looking at a beautiful opportunity and every red flag that could pop up did, but I would justify it by saying, "Why would God open this door, if it is not the way?"

There are so many instances where God spoke through circumstances in the Bible. The truth of the matter is, in every circumstance, when we look back, we have instances where God has spoken, and we **knew** it was God. We just struggled to trust His voice. We would rather listen to the many voices screaming in our thoughts and mind and all the people around us that are saying different.

God used the prophet, Ezekiel in Ezekiel 4 to prophesy physically to a people who were, in that time, too stubborn to listen. Ezekiel literally laid on his left side for 390 days and his right side for 40 days to prophesy physically what would happen to the people of Israel. God used circumstances to prophesy to Israel because their heart was hardened, they would not listen, and they were a stubborn people.

At times in our life, God will do the very same.

He will use the circumstances around us to confirm to us everything that He has been speaking within us. He will use the things that He warned us against to show us that it is **He** who is God and who we should trust in **all** things. Yet, even in those times, God does not leave us. He is always there even if it seems He is silent.

> "If God is not speaking, He could be teaching."
> ~Jeanice Sherai

God speaks through people

Sometimes we seek God repeatedly for understanding in a situation and it seems we are receiving no guidance. Then out of the blue, there is a random person we join in conversation with at the grocery store and they say something so random but so fitting to what we are dealing with, that we know it has to be God. Sometimes God speaks through a mentor, a pastor, or even through a friend.

At any time, God can use people as His vessel to get a message to us.

God knows what we need. I can remember so many times I would sit in prayer with God and when I look up from praying, there was a text on my phone speaking to the very thing I prayed about. I can remember a time when I lost a job that I loved due to company downsizing. I had planned my whole life at that job y'all, but God **had other plans**. I remember being so devastated as if God had not previously prepared me for such as time a this.

Yet I can admit that when I look back, God had spoken to me many times through circumstances and people that change was coming, but I would not **listen**. It was not what I wanted and so I continued to pray to God for something different.

I remember flying home from vacation and something telling me to buy the book, "Who moved my cheese?"

This book was all about change and how different personalities react to change. This book was sooo good, but I refused to believe what I knew within me...this book was speaking directly to me. I had a plan. I wanted God on board with my plan, so I used my faith to see if God would listen to my will instead of His. Now that is a deep truth y'all, but we know who's will, will always win.

When I was laid off from my job, there were so many blessings in the transition, but I did not want them. I wanted to keep working in that place and live out the plans that I personally had made. I was so down and depressed and I can remember my husband telling me to quit mourning a place that God had removed me from and celebrate where I am going. I was so angry with him because I did not want truth in that place, I wanted to go back to what I had lost. Yet, that was not God's plan for me, and He had spoken it through so many different people.

Every sermon I listened to spoke of the Israelites leaving Egypt and walking into their promised land. I heard these messages, I knew it was God, but I still prayed for Him to change His mind.

> "I was caught up in what I had planned, and God was caught up in what He had promised me in my life."
> **~Jeanice Sherai**

Have you ever experienced this before? Every single person around you was speaking the same message. Within your soul, you knew what they were saying resonated through you, but you still rejected it because it was not the truth you wanted to hear. I heard a coach say recently, "The message or the sermon we hear is the milk, but it is when we take time to truly meditate on that Word and hear what God is speaking to us, that it becomes meat and truly sustains us." Whew!!

How powerful is that? Anyone can speak into our life, but until we take that Word to God and truly dig deep into what He is speaking specifically to us, it will not be sustaining.

When God speaks through people, it is not their interpretation of the Word that they spoke that we need, it is God's meaning that we need. We need a Word that sustains us and so we must take that spoken Word to God and ask Him what does this Word mean specifically for my life.

It is that personal understanding that will be the meat that will sustain us in the toughest of places.

When I stopped rejecting what God was speaking and started listening, I felt God literally shift my body. I went from looking at what was behind me, to what He said was before me in my life. I could literally see a vision of Him turning my body to **only** look forward and that in itself is a vision that **still** sustains me until this very day.

God speaks through Dreams

I know many of us think that our dream life at night is so far fetch that we rarely pay attention to what we are dreaming anymore. Yet, one of the primary ways that

God spoke in the Bible was in the form of dreams. He spoke to believers and non-believers through dreams.

Just take a look at the story of Joseph. God not only spoke to Joseph through dreams, but he used his gift of dream interpretation to elevate him to a place where he could help his family when a famine was approaching (Genesis 37 -50).

God spoke to many Kings through dreams and those Kings would be directed almost every time to a chosen vessel of God to interpret those dreams.

God will not only speak through dreams, but He also will give us understanding through dreams. We have to discern however, if those dreams are from God, if those dreams are our subconscious, or if they are from the enemy. So, the first thing we can do when we awaken from a dream is seek God and ask Him: *"God was this dream a message from you?"*

How can we tell when a dream is from God? We can ask wise and trusted counsel about the dream. We can take time to assess the dream. Most importantly, we can pray and seek God concerning that dream.

The understanding of dreams is a gift, but that does not mean it is a gift that God will not give us if we ask Him for it. The understanding of dreams can also not be taught in just one chapter of this book. You will have to do your research and study the many different dreams in the Bible in order to fully understand the gift of interpreting dreams. You will have to study books from Christian writers who teach about dreams and how God speaks to Christians in dreams. There is a lot to be understood about dreams, but most of it can truly be learned through the examples that God has already provided in His Word and how they sought God for understanding.

Here are some things we can ask about our dreams:

Did the dream make me afraid? God's Word says that, "He has not given us a spirit of fear (2 Timothy 1:7)."

Did the dream portray thoughts that I have been having lately or right before I fell asleep? Sometimes these dreams are just a subconscious form of what is going on in our mind during the day.

Did the dream give me direction, wisdom, or warning? This could very well be a dream from God.

I always pay attention to symbolism in dreams because that is what God used to convey the meaning of dreams in the Bible.

For example, I truly believe that numbers in a dream could have importance if the dream is from God. If there are three people around me in a dream, I know that it is from God, and I know God is present.

If there are reoccurrences of the same dream over and over again, then I begin to pay attention to what God could be speaking to me or what I have not **released** from my subconscious thoughts.

I also pay attention to colors in my dreams when they are from God. How could God be speaking to me through this color represented in my dream? What does this color mean?

I pay attention more to what the items in my dream personally represent to me more than I do definitions, books, or any other thing concerning those items in my dream.

I pay attention to the people in my dreams that are from God. What does their name mean? What is their current character or mannerisms in real life? How do I feel about this person in real life?

Often, our dreams are God showing us **ourselves**, *even* if it involves other people.

Yet sometimes there is a case, when we dream and the entire time it is like we are watching a person or situation from a different view, in those times, God is giving us insight into that person and how we can pray for them via that dream.

Jesus often spoke in parables in the Bible and in our

dreams, He will do the very same.

I dream often and one day I plan to write a more in-depth book about dreams, but until then I hope this helps you to know that God can definitely speak through your dreams.

Take a moment to look at an example dream and then I want you to practice with a dream you have had recently.

Example Dream:

> "Last night I dreamed that there was a football game on the TV. I was so intrigued with this game and as I watched, I was in a dark room sitting on the couch. Then my dad walked in the room and turned the light on and He asked what was the score. I told him we were winning. He responded, "Good," and closed the door.

Questions I would ask myself:

Is this dream from God?
Once I have confirmation that this dream is indeed one that is pointing out something to me, edifying me, giving me direction, or simply bearing the fruits of the spirit, I move forward to understand what God is speaking.

What am I doing in the dream?
Watching a Football Game

What emotion am I feeling?
Intrigued, focused, and engrossed in what is taking place.

Anything else standing out in the dream?
I was sitting in the dark and my dad turned the light on.

Who was in the dream?
My dad.

What is his character in your life?
He is my father. A person I can depend on. A voice of reason. A man of few words. A man with wisdom.

How does this relate in life?
I am currently focused on a battle in my life. I could not shift my focus and had become engrossed with what was taking place. It was causing me to feel defeated and had placed me in a dark place.

What do you believe God showed you?
He gave me light (insight) on my battle. When he came in the room, he turned on the light and then asked me a question. I immediately knew that we had the victory and I told him.

What is the message?
The battle that has taken my attention is already won. Trust God and shift my focus and my mindset from a dark place to one of victory.

Have you had a dream recently? Do you believe it was a dream from God? If so, take time to write it down. Ask yourself the questions I went through for the example dream above. Do not be hard on yourself. If you cannot figure out the meaning, give God time. Often, we may discover the meaning in its fullness later and we will see then that that is exactly what we dreamed and what God meant.

The more we sit with God and ask for His wisdom, the more He supplies it.

"To those who listen to my teaching, more understanding will be given, and they will have an abundance of knowledge. But for those who are not listening, even what little understanding they have will be taken away from them."
Matthew 13:12 NLT

Your Dream:

_____

_____

_____

_____

_____

_____

Now Break it Down:

What were you doing?

_____

_____

What were your emotions?

_____

_____

What stood out in the dream?

_____

_____

Who was in the dream?

_____

_____

What is their character?

_____

_____

_____

How does this relate in life?

_____

_____

_____

What is God showing you?

_____

_____

_____

What is His message?

_____

_____

_____

God speaks in many ways throughout the Bible. In this chapter, I have only mentioned a few of those ways. I encourage you to take time to study even more concerning God's voice, so that you will **know** when it is God.

> When you are walking through life and God keeps showing up through signs, sermons, and circumstances with a repeated message. That is how you will KNOW that it is God.

When desiring to hear God, we must try our hardest to not place Him in a box. We must give God the space and room to show up in our life in the way He desires.

That is how we will develop a personal relationship with God. **This is how we will know when it is God.**

References of God Speaking to His Children in the Bible	
Individual	*Scripture*
Moses	*Exodus 3*
Job	*Job 38*
Judah	*Isaiah 30*
Ezekiel	*Ezekiel 4*
Joseph	*Genesis 37*

FINAL WORDS

"We won't ever have the fullest confirmation that it is God, but we will have His hints along the way that this is the direction He is leading. No matter what, God will never leave us. It's a faith walk for a reason."
~Jeanice Sherai

I wish that I could wrap this book up with a surety to you that in every decision you make, you will **know** that it is God. The truth is, God leads us "by faith and not by sight (2 Corinthians 5:7)" just as His word promises.

We may not ever truly **know** in times if it was God, but as we walk forward, I promise that He will step in and lead you along the way. God's Word promises that when we get off track, He will leave the ninety-nine to find us (Matthew 18:12) and I don't know about you, but for me that is the **most** comforting promise to hear.

I often tell people to pay attention to how they feel within. Do you feel rushed? Do you feel anger? Do you feel chaos and confusion?

> Paying attention to the emotions around what you are hearing, is key to helping you know when it is God. You will know when it is Him you are following or Him that is redirecting you as you walk through this life by listening to what you are experiencing within.

That is why I believe that meditating on God's Word is so important. The more we learn to be still before God and truly listen, the more we will begin to know when it is truly Him. The more you know God's Word, the more you will recognize when it is God.

I pray that this book has been and will continue to be the reference tool that you have needed to truly trust and know when it is God. I pray that it has helped you in believing in what you are hearing and trusting God with the direction He desires to give you.

I pray that as you have read each chapter, you began to take step after step in **faith**.

How will you know when it is God? Get moving.

Move in the direction God is calling and trust Him to steer you as you continue to step in the direction you believe within that you should take.

ABOUT THE AUTHOR

Jeanice Durrah is a believer of Jesus Christ. She is the wife to her loving husband, Victor Durrah, Jr and the mother to their sweet daughter, Victory. She hopes that through her life experiences she can be a light to others paths who are traveling along in life and learning to lean and depend on God. You can learn more about her mission on her website: www.jeanicesherai.com.

Made in the USA
Columbia, SC
15 November 2022